Celebrations and Choice Makers

Stan Campbell and Carol Smith

David C. Cook Publishing Co.

Elgin, Illinois/Weston, Ontario

SNAP SESSIONS: *Celebrations and Choice Makers*

© 1993 David C. Cook Publishing Co.

PUBLISHED BY

David C. Cook Publishing Co.
850 N. Grove Ave., Elgin, IL 60120
Cable address: DCCOOK

DESIGNED BY
Tabb Associates

INTERIOR ILLUSTRATIONS BY
Keith Locke

COVER ILLUSTRATION BY
Gary Locke

ADDITIONAL MATERIAL BY
Lorraine Triggs

Printed in U.S.A.

ISBN: 0-7814-5052-7

CONTENTS

Are You Too Busy to Read This Introduction?

It's 5:30 on a Sunday night. You're panicking. Your next youth group meeting is just 30 minutes away—and you aren't ready! In fact, you've been so busy this week that you haven't really gotten *anything* together for this meeting!

Sweat pops from your forehead as you flip through the programming resources on your shelf. But the typical meeting plan you find there requires you to gather a crate of eggplants and a parachute, cut 50 index cards into two-inch squares, and round up a panel of guest speakers. There's no time for that!

Some plans on your shelf are simpler, but require you to photocopy reproducible student sheets—and you don't have quick access to a copier. And since your group's meeting outside, you don't have a chalkboard, either.

What are you going to do? If only there were some books of *really* easy-to-prepare youth meetings, sessions that you could read and put together at top speed!

Now there are! The *Snap Sessions* series is designed specifically for busy youth workers—which includes practically all of us!

The Simple Truth

What's so great about a Snap Session? Simple: It's simple!

• To lead a Snap Session, you *never need more than Bibles, pencils, paper, and a household object!* There's no photocopying or cutting or pasting or rehearsing, either!

• It's easy to grasp each session plan at a glance. Instructions to you are in regular type; things you could say to the group are in bold type; suggested answers are in parentheses.

• Despite the ease of preparation, meetings are full-length (45-60 minutes) and full-strength (creative, active, and relating the Bible to kids' lives).

• If you have extra preparation time, you can dress the meeting up with optional, more involved activities listed at the end of each session.

We could go on and on about *Snap Sessions*—but we know you don't have time. Grab one of the 30 sessions that follow and get going! Your group members are ready for a great meeting—and you're about to give them one!

—Randy Southern, Series Editor

Fall Kickoff

BIG IDEA

Whenever we expect to face new, different, or difficult circumstances, we need to set some personal standards ahead of time.

BIBLE INPUT

Daniel 1

BRING:

Bibles
Pencils
Paper
Football

1 Have a Kicking Competition

Since this is a fall kickoff, see how well group members can kick. If you can get outdoors, use a football and give each person two or three tries to punt for distance, and then to place kick for distance. In each case, let each person stand where his or her kick lands. Then, to make things interesting, have the guys go back and try again, using the foot they didn't use the first time. Make sure the girls remain, and see how many of the guys can exceed those distances. (If you don't have the opportunity to do this outside, either improvise a similar activity inside with a paper football, or play circle soccer. [See Optional Extra #3.])

2 Write Some Cheers

Divide into small groups and ask each group to create a cheer or cheers to present to the group as a whole. Just as cheerleaders try to rouse the spectators at a football game, these cheers should foster encouragement or confidence of (spiritual) victory. (Later in the session you will be setting some goals for this school year. Perhaps some of your small groups will first identify a goal and then create a cheer to address the goal. However, many are more likely to simply adapt existing cheers used at their schools.)

If this exercise works well, consider using the better cheers on a regular basis. You might even want to divide future meetings into four "quarters" like a football game. You can make announcements at "halftime," or give a "two-minute warning" toward the end of the meeting. Try to maintain some of the opening night excitement as you go through the year.

3 Get to Know Each Other Better

Seat group members in a circle with one person holding the football. Ask a question that requires an opinion or reveals something about the person answering, such as:
- When do you get the most nervous?
- Who are two of your personal heroes?
- What do you anticipate will be your biggest challenge this year?
- If you could visit anywhere in the world for a week, where would you go? Why?

After you ask a question, have the person with the football toss it to the group member he would like to have answer the question. Then ask the next question and let the person who answered toss the ball to someone else. Continue until everyone has responded to at least one question.

4 Stressful Situations

Ask: **How many of you feel fully prepared for this new school year?** Let group members discuss why they are ready (or not ready) for what lies ahead.

Look at Daniel 1 and compare Daniel's experience with that of your students going into a new year where they may not feel very secure. Have someone read Daniel 1:1-7, and then discuss:

• **How do you think you would respond if an enemy nation suddenly rolled into our city and took control (including carrying off everything valuable in our church)?**

• **Do you think you would have been chosen as part of Daniel's group to be carried off? Why?** (Note that these were the best and brightest of the Hebrew people.)

• **If you *were* chosen, would you have wanted to go? Why or why not?** (Contrast the trauma of being taken away from home with the "perks" of working for the king.)

• **The name changes of Daniel and his friends were probably to honor Babylonian gods. What are some situations where *we* change other people's names in a way that dishonors God?** (Discuss the tendency of young people to give cruel nicknames to others.)

Have someone read Daniel 1:8-14 and continue the discussion:

• **What major problem did Daniel face in his transition?** (His new life-style—his diet in particular—violated his personal religious standards.)

• **How did Daniel deal with his problem?** (By deciding *ahead of time* what he could not do in good conscience. Yet he wasn't combative in his dealings with his captors. He politely worked out an alternative agreeable to everyone. Also point out that Daniel's proposed "test" certainly required faith.)

Finally, have someone read Daniel 1:15-21. Discuss:

• **How did Daniel's test turn out? Why?** (Devotion to God is always rewarded sooner or later. In this case, it was sooner. God provided Daniel, Shadrach, Meshach, and Abednego not only with health, but also with special wisdom and insight—ten times as much as the others.)

• **How might this story apply to you?** (As we enter *any* new and possibly frightening experience, we should establish certain ground rules based on our Christian beliefs *before* we are pressured to compromise. And we can be confident that God will reward our faithfulness to Him by remaining faithful to us.)

5 *Set Goals for the Year to Come*

Ask group members to think of some goals they would be willing to work toward during this school year. Some might closely parallel those of Daniel, such as not to be "defiled" by alcohol or drugs. Others may not be related to the story at all (such as sexual purity, a stronger spirit of unity, an increased quickness to forgive one another, etc.). If all, or at least a vast majority of group members, are willing to commit to specific goals, write these out on a sheet of paper and post it in a prominent place. Later, perhaps someone can copy the list on a piece of poster board. But be sure these agreed-to goals remain in clear sight throughout the school year. They will be constant reminders that we serve a powerful and faithful God who we need to trust in times of stress.

Optional Extras

1. *Go As a Group.* Plan to attend at least one school football game as a group to increase a spirit of unity.

2. *Game Ball.* Use a football as a "game ball." Give it to students who accomplish specific spiritual goals during the school year.

3. *Circle Soccer.* Seat kids in chairs in a circle. Half the circle is Team A and the other half is Team B. The object of the game is to stay seated and kick a soccer ball (below the shoulders) between the chairs of the opposite team.

Welcoming New Members

BIG IDEA — Inviting new people to the youth group and making them feel welcome should be an ongoing priority.

BIBLE INPUT — John 1:35-51

BRING:
Bibles
Pencils
Paper
Name tags

1 Discover Your Secret Identity

Before the meeting, prepare some self-adhesive name tags with the names of famous people (past or present, real or fictional). As group members arrive, place one of the name tags on each person's back without letting him or her see the name. Then have everyone try to figure out his or her character by asking yes-or-no questions to other people. However, no one may ask more than one question of *anyone* until he has asked at least one question to *everyone*. And no one may make more than one guess after asking a question. The purpose of this activity is to encourage kids to mix with new people in a nonthreatening way.

When group members finally guess their secret identities, remove the tags from their backs and have them wear them on the front to help identify those who still need to ask questions. Try to choose characters that your students relate well to, such as Michael Jordan, Luke Perry, Marcia Brady, "Beaver" Cleaver, Michael Jackson, etc.

2 Prepare Genuine Name Tags

Give each person another name tag. In addition to their names, ask everyone to include three symbols that reflect their interests, hobbies, family life, job, or similar involvement. Make sure they write their first names in large letters so other people—especially new ones—can easily identify them. When everyone has finished, have them wear their tags for the rest of the session.

3 Conduct an Information Circle

Seat kids in a circle. Explain that you want to get to know each other better, so each person should fill in the blanks and say, "I'm _____ and I like _____." The first person might say, "I'm John and I like playing football." The next person then says, "He's John. He likes playing football. I'm Angie and I like Rocky Road ice cream." Each person in turn is responsible for remembering one additional statement. (Try to let your new people participate early in the circle. The others will be more knowledgeable of each other's names and interests.) If someone forgets, start the circle again. But it's surprising how easy it is to learn names and a little about everyone in the group in a single sitting. (Very large groups may need to divide into smaller, but still challenging, circles.)

4 The New Kid in the Group

If you have not yet done so, officially welcome your new people. Explain the purpose of your group and describe some of the recent activities you've done. Some new people may feel threatened at first because of incorrect perceptions of church or Christianity. Do all you can to put them at ease.

Discuss: **How do you feel when you're in a totally new situation and aren't quite sure what to do or how to act?** (Call on some of the regular members to respond.) **Do you enjoy new experiences, or are you very uncomfortable? If you were reluctant to come to this group, what factors might influence your decision?** (Knowing someone there; going with a friend; expecting the rewards to be greater than the initial discomfort; etc.) **What would determine whether or not you came back?** (Stress that the way new people are treated by individual members is usually far more influential than the program, teaching, etc.)

Ask group members to listen as you read John 1:35-51. Then discuss:

• **How many disciples did Jesus have to begin with?** (None. However, John the Baptist had disciples who were preparing the way for Jesus.)

• **How do you think John's disciples felt when they left him to talk to Jesus?**

• **How much do you know about Andrew?** (Very little. But contrast this to all we know about Peter. Note that Andrew was responsible for Peter meeting Jesus.)

• **Was everyone impressed with Jesus?** (Not at first. Nathanael was a real skeptic until Jesus revealed one small indication of His insight. But when He did, Nathanael was quick to believe.)

If group members haven't yet made the following observations, summarize:

• **A good way to handle being new in a group is to bring someone even newer.**

• **We know at least two of Jesus' original disciples met Him because of someone else (Andrew brought Peter; Philip brought Nathanael).**

• **Jesus didn't mind when these "new" people asked silly questions or even that they doubted He was anyone special.**

• **We don't have to memorize the Bible before we invite others to the group. We just need to know three words: "Come and see."**

• **Whether you're new or a long-established member, we don't know all the surprises God has in store for us. The original disciples could not have even begun to imagine where this new relationship with Jesus would eventually lead.**

5 Prepare to Follow Up

Before your new members leave, pass around a sheet of paper (or use remaining name tags) for each new person present. Everyone else should sign the paper or name tag and add anything else they would be willing to do for the person who is new to the group meeting. For example, one person might write down a phone number with the comment, "Give me a call if you just want to talk." Someone might write, "My dad owns the pie shop and I can get us free samples." Others could offer to study together or provide rides to school. When finished, give the sheets of paper or name tags to your new people.

If new people truly feel welcome in your group, they will keep coming back. And as the personal relationships grow stronger, they will provide better, more natural opportunities for spiritual growth to take place as well.

Optional Extras

1. *Progressive Dinner.* Plan a progressive dinner to get new people into members' homes, not just the church.

2. *Q & A Meeting.* If lots of new people are coming to your group, you may want to consider asking your pastor to lead a meeting or two where he can answer questions concerning God, the church, doctrine, etc.

3. *Face-to-Face.* Instead of using name tags in Step 1, use actual pictures of people taken from newspapers or magazines. Make sure the characters are easily identifiable. Good sources would include teen magazines, newspaper comics, and TV Guides. After all identities have been guessed, have kids get into groups of three or four. Each group should develop a plausible reason for why their characters are popular, and either explain it to the rest of the group or present a short skit.

Parents Night

BIG IDEA Though adolescence is frequently a period of rebellion, both parents and teenagers can strengthen and cherish their relationship.

BIBLE INPUT Ephesians 6:1-9

BRING: Pencils
Paper
Envelopes

1 Make Introductions

Some kids might not be too thrilled about a parents night. Let kids know that every parent is welcomed—two parents, single parents, older parents, and parents who may not know the Lord. If some kids' parents don't come, get these kids involved in helping lead this session. For example, one kid could welcome everyone to the session. Another kid could explain the activity.

Begin your meeting with a spirit of a political convention. Let kids introduce their parents in as eloquent (or at least long-winded) ways as they can. You might begin by introducing the other group leaders: **Ladies and gentlemen, I want you to meet the best associate youth group leader this world has ever seen. . . . A (wo)man whose love for young people far outweighs his (her) common sense, as was attested two weeks ago during "Pie in the Face" Night. A person who spends hours each week preparing for our meetings, and even longer recovering after each one. Here's John/Joan Smith!** (Cue applause.)

Have each group member introduce his or her parents in a similar manner, including information such as careers, hobbies, special talents, favorite foods, nicknames, and so forth. After each introduction, give the parent a rousing round of applause and cheers.

2 Let Parents Share Secrets

Since parents were somewhat at the mercy of their kids during the introductions, reverse the situation a bit. Provide paper and pencils to parents and have them share a piece of information about their children that perhaps the rest of the group doesn't know, yet would find interesting. Each parent should begin, "One time my child . . ." and at the bottom, write the name of his or her child. Collect the papers, mix them up, and read one at a time. See how well kids can identify the "culprit" in each story. By reading the papers yourself, you can screen any you feel might be *too* embarrassing or humiliating. In such a case, you could either ask the parent for a different event, or simply not get around to reading all of them.

3 Express Hopes for the Future

Next provide paper for everyone—both parents and group members. Instruct everyone to complete two sentences: (1) "The best things about our family are . . ." and (2) "What I wish was different about our family is. . . ." Encourage everyone to provide as many responses to both statements as they would like. Assure them that they need not include their names, so they can be completely honest. Collect the papers and read them randomly. First read through each of the responses for the first statement. See what the parents and kids feel is being done right in families. Parents can learn from other kids through this method. (If they aren't spending much time with their own children but discover that a number of others note that as a "best thing," they'll get the message.)

Move on to the "wish list" of improvements that could be made in current family relationships. Don't linger too long on any single statement. Move through them quickly so the group remains focused on what is being said rather than trying to guess who said it. Again, the expression of one person is likely to apply to many of the families represented.

4 Goals for Parents and Children

Explain that you are going to cover only one short biblical passage today. Then quote: **"Children, obey your parents in the Lord, for this is right"** (Ephesians 6:1). Ask: **How many of you like this verse?** (Use a show of hands to see if most parents respond and most young people don't.) **How many of you have done something during the past week that might have violated this biblical instruction?** (Again, wait for show of hands. Check for adults as well, because many of them will still have living parents.) **Why do so many of us have trouble following this clear and simple statement?** (Let kids and parents respond. If they begin to offer excuses, so much the better. Don't resist at this point.)

Then explain that you aren't through with the passage you referred to. Continue by reading Ephesians 6:2, 3. Discuss: **Why do you think God made "Honor your father and mother" one of the Ten Commandments?** (Families are important to Him. Children are to respect the God-given authority of their parents for their own personal benefit and for the strength of society as a whole.) **What does obeying parents have to do with things "going well" and "enjoying long life on the earth"?** (Have kids name potentially harmful things that young people do when they don't follow parental instructions: drinking, drug experimentation, sexual activity, dangerous driving, and so forth.)

Explain that you still aren't finished with the passage. Read Ephesians 6:4. Again ask: **How many of you have experienced something during the past week that might have violated this biblical instruction?** (Ask for a show of hands.) Challenge parents to develop a deeper level of patience with their children. Then point out that the two commands go hand in hand. If children are honoring their parents, the adults probably won't exasperate their kids as easily or as often. And if the parents are a bit more understanding and trusting, the children should show their gratitude by honoring them.

Ask: **What if you don't really have a good parent/child relationship to begin with? What if the young person feels more like a slave than a child?** (Let group members respond.) Then say that you haven't finished the passage. Paul may have been dealing with the same question as he wrote the Ephesians. Explain that Christians in the early church had some unusual relationships. Occasionally, both slaves and masters would become Christians. So they might go to church on Sunday and relate to each other as Christian brothers, but during the rest of the week the slave was still a slave and the master was still a master—perhaps the way it may seem between parents and children in some families.

Read Ephesians 6:5-9. Discuss: **What should both parents and children remember as they relate to each other?** (Both are responsible to God for their actions. God rewards faithfulness, even if we don't receive respect from other family members. If even slaves and masters were accountable for their behavior and attitudes, most of us should probably try harder to maintain stronger family relationships.)

5 Draft Commitment Sheets

Hand out pencils, paper, and blank envelopes. In response to the passage in Ephesians and the discussion, have everyone think of at least one thing in their parent/child relationships that could stand some improvement. When they get a specific rough spot in mind, have them make a commitment to work on it during the next three months. They should write out their specific intent and sign it: "During the next three months, I commit to working on. . . ."

No one should disclose his or her commitment. It should be between himself or herself and God. As kids and parents finish, ask them to seal their commitments in an envelope and address it to themselves. Collect the envelopes, and plan to mail them out in three months. Close with a prayer for the young people, for the parents, and for God's acceptance of each of us on equal status as *His* children.

Remember to follow up with a discussion on whether they abided by their commitments, or if the commitments were quickly forgotten.

Optional Extras

1. *Baby Pictures.* In advance, ask parents to bring baby pictures of group members (without the knowledge of the people in the group). Post the pictures in a prominent place and see how many people can be correctly identified.

2. *Kids Cook.* If you have risk-taking group members and brave parents, include in this session a special dinner for the parents—prepared by the group members.

DATE USED

Birthday

BIG IDEA

While the annual anniversary of our physical birth is a traditional reason to celebrate, we can be even more excited about our spiritual rebirth.

BIBLE INPUT

II Peter 3:8
Matthew 18:1-6

BRING:

Bibles
Paper
Journal or diary

1 Introduce with a Mad Lib

Before celebrating the birthdays, have group members call out words to fit the categories listed in parentheses below. As they do, write them into the spaces without revealing the purpose. When you have filled in all the slots, say: **We are here today to honor John** (or whomever). **To begin with, I've done some extensive research into John's background, and I want to tell you about him.**

Be sure to replace the person's name for the name "John", adjusting the gender if necessary. Be sensitive to the specific person's feelings. (If, for instance, he has some kind of physical problem, leave out the sentences about the body building.)

John was born in a little (*Adjective*) cabin in (*Place*). He weighed (*Number*) pounds at birth, and his parents were so very (*Adjective*). As a child, he liked to (*Verb*), (*Verb*), and (*Verb*), like most small children do. His biggest dream was to be a (*Profession*), so in school he spent a lot of time in (*School Subject*) class. He developed a crush on (*Female/Male Teacher at School*), but got over it when he met (*Female/Male Person in Room*).

John's hard work in school has earned him a (*Letter of Alphabet*)-minus average. He is also proud of the shape he is in. Just by looking, you can tell he works out to build up his (*Part of the Body*). If you ask for his philosophy of life, he will tell you, (*Popular Phrase*).

We all think John is pretty special. He's faster than a speeding (*Noun*), more powerful than a (*Noun*), and able to leap tall (*Plural Noun*) in a single bound. Today, as we celebrate his (*Number*)th birthday, we wish him all the (*Plural Noun*) in the world. As the song goes: (*Adjective*) birthday to you. (*Adjective*) birthday to you. (*Adjective*) birthday, dear John. (*Adjective*) birthday to you.

2 Write a Better Birthday Song

Divide into groups and let each group work on an original birthday song for the person whose birthday it is—even if the best they can do is "We Wish You a Happy Birthday" to the tune of "We Wish You a Merry Christmas." When they are ready, let each group sing its song to the honoree.

3 Describe the Ideal Age

Let each group member describe the perfect age, or simply ask, "Which birthday is the best one?" Younger members may focus on the magic sixteen, when they are finally able to drive. Some might be looking toward eighteen when they can vote or graduate. Some kids are likely to have friends who can hardly wait until they're the legal drinking age. Challenge your group to go beyond the "entitlements" of certain ages, and dwell instead on the experiences. For example, they may be able to vote at age eighteen, but their parents may expect them to have full-time summer jobs by then. Would it be better to choose the age of the last free summer? Or the year the person gets married (regardless of the age)? Or the year when the family is still completely together, before members move out on their own?

4 The Most Important Birthday

Ask: **About how old do you think God is?** (This is a trick question, of course, but see if anyone responds with "billions and billions of years old." Explain that the passing of time is something we experience, but God doesn't. God has always existed and always will. While we measure our existence in years, there is no such measurement we can use for God.)

To make the point, have someone read II Peter 3:8. Discuss:

• **Do you think this is a literal translation of time: One day =1,000 years?** (No. It's a comparison. As days can pass quickly for us, so do millennia for God.)

• **What point do you think Peter is trying to make?** (See verse 9. God is not limited by time. We may think He is sometimes slow to act, but in our impatience we don't see His great level of patience.)

Have someone read John 3:1-8. Discuss:

• **How do you think God feels about our birthdays?** (He personally was involved with our actual birth [Psalm 139:13-16], and if we celebrate His creation of us along with each birthday, we honor Him. However, to simply mark the years and not recognize God's involvement in our lives is a hollow celebration.)

• **Why does Jesus put so much emphasis on being born again?** (We are born physically into sin. Until we are reborn spiritually, we cannot experience life as God intends it for us. Our spiritual rebirth [being "born again"] is more important than simply marking the years of life.)

• **In what ways can we celebrate our spiritual "birthdays"?** (Some people mark the day and celebrate annually. But more important, whether or not we know the specific date, we should celebrate every day.)

Have someone read Matthew 18:1-6. Discuss:

• **What are some ways that young people try to show they are maturing?**

(Perhaps smoking, being sexually active, drinking, getting a part-time job.)

• **What challenge does Jesus give us as we grow older?** (We are to be like little children.)

• **Do you think Jesus is telling us to remain childish—to argue over toys, cry when we don't get our way? Explain.** (We are to "put *childish* ways behind" [I Corinthians 13:11]. Yet Jesus praises *childlike* qualities such as a trusting faith in God, submission to authority, lack of prejudice, etc.)

• **Which do you think is harder—starting to drink and hanging with the group who wants to act "grown up," or leading a life where you care most about pleasing God? Explain.**

Challenge group members, as they celebrate birthdays, not to overdo the emphasis on being able to do certain things. Encourage them to live each day as a celebration of what God has already done for them—and for what He continues to do.

5 Begin a Celebration Journal

Start a celebration journal (a diary or blank book) for your group. Note today's date and the person's birthday. Let everyone sign the page and record something your group did today, something about the birthday person, or similar comments. If you wish, include prayer requests. Bring the journal every time you have a celebration: holidays, retreats, or special events. Before long you will have a special history of your group.

Close with a special prayer for the person celebrating the birthday, and for the new birth God makes possible for everyone.

Optional Extras

1. *Birthday Bash. Instead* of celebrating one person's birthday, adapt the session to celebrate everyone's birthday. Use the mad lib in Step 1 to honor the person who has a birthday closest to today. After Step 5, serve birthday cake (with candles) and ice cream.

2. *Birthday Games.* Play children's party games with slight twists. For example, instead of "Pin the Tail on the Donkey," see which team can blow up the most balloons in five minutes and stuff them inside a team member wearing long underwear (or loose-fitting sweats). Count the total by popping them with a pin while team members count off. Use your imagination for other similar games.

New Believer

BIG IDEA

The salvation of a friend or family member is the best possible reason to celebrate. In such cases, not only do we rejoice, but so do God and His angels.

BIBLE INPUT

Luke 15:1-24

BRING:

Bibles
Pencils
Paper
Dollar bills or coins

1 Hold a Treasure Hunt

Before the meeting, hide some money at several places around the room. (If ten *silver* dollars won't break your budget, use them so you can better tie in the treasure hunt with the Bible study later on. In any case, the value should be high enough to command interest, and the quantity should be sufficient so that all the money is not found too soon.) Be sure a few of the pieces of money are *very* well hidden and will require a diligent search. Let people who find the money keep it.

2 Hold a Person Hunt

While the treasure hunt is taking place, have an adult leader hide somewhere that will be very difficult to find (perhaps in a car in the parking lot). As group members find the last of the money, comment that a leader is missing. Form a search party and send everyone out to look. Observe the degree to which they get involved. After your missing person is found, reassemble and discuss: **Did you put more effort into finding the money or the person? Why?**

See if group members realize that they may tend to be more thorough if there is some kind of personal payoff in store for them. Do they place more value on materialistic things than on human relationships? When *people* are lost, do they leave it up to others to look for them? You might want to make parallels when you get to the Luke 15 passage.

3 Recall the Feeling of Being Lost

Ask group members to talk about times when they were lost, or when they lost something valuable. Discuss their experiences:
   • **Did you ever get lost as a child? What happened? How did you feel?**
   • **As you've started driving, have you ever ended up in some strange place you didn't intend to? What thoughts were going through your head?**
   • **What is the most valuable thing you thought you lost, but eventually found? How did you feel while it was missing? How did you find your lost item?**
   • **Have you ever lost something permanently? What emotions did you experience after you decided it would never be found? How do you feel about it *now*?**

What words do your young people use in regard to personal lostness, or lost possessions? (Panic? Fear? Despair?) They might come to the conclusion that the value of the lost object (in terms of personal worth) helps to determine the extent and intensity of the feelings.

God's Lost and Found

Divide into three groups and have each group study one of the parables in Luke 15, each of which involves something that is lost. Have each group answer the same set of questions:

1. **What was the thing that was lost?**
2. **What percent of the total did the lost item make up?**
3. **To what extent did the owner (or father) try to get it back?**
4. **What was the emotional state of the person upon regaining the item that was originally lost?**

Here are the assignments, as well as possible discoveries of each group.

Luke 15:1-7

The lost item was a sheep—one of one hundred. Yet even though it was only one percent of the shepherd's flock, it was important for him to find it. He made a point to go and search for it. He was joyful when he found his lost sheep, so much so that he threw a party to celebrate.

Luke 15:8-10

A woman lost one of ten silver coins. (Each coin was worth about a day's wages.) This ten percent of her savings was important to her. She didn't look around casually. Rather, she lit a lamp, grabbed a broom, and made every effort to find her lost coin. When she finally did, she too hosted a party for her friends and neighbors.

Luke 15:11-24

This story is perhaps the most gripping, because the prodigal son was lost by his own decision. Having turned his back on home and family, he chose a life-style that quickly used up his money. Consequently, he lost his friends as well. The lostness of this person became more a loss of direction and purpose than a literal geographic lostness. The father had another son at home, but fifty percent was certainly not what the father hoped for. Yet it was interesting that he patiently waited rather than going after his lost son. He knew that the son left on his own accord, and must choose to return the same way. When the son eventually repented and went back home, the father was overjoyed. He first hugged and kissed him. Then he provided a robe, a ring, a feast, and a celebration.

When all the groups have reported, discuss:

• **What do these parables symbolize?** (They all show God's intense concern for those who are lost.)

• **What percentage does God want to respond to His love and concern?** (His desire is for *everyone* to be "found." [See II Peter 3:9.] Even with ninety-nine percent in the "fold," He will still seek out the remaining one percent. Percentages don't really matter. Each individual is loved by God, and He wants all to be saved.)

• **If we are in danger of eternal lostness, why doesn't God just zap us back to Him?** (God does make the first move, but He also wants us to respond.)

• In what ways are you like the shepherd, the woman, or the father when it comes to your dealings with people who are lost?

5 Encourage New Believers

Officially welcome any formerly "lost" people into the group as new believers. Then have other group members offer words of wisdom about what to expect. Some might want to share times God has felt especially close. Some might want to tell what they have done to maintain a regular discipline of spiritual growth. Some might even be willing to share some of the rough spots they have faced since becoming a Christian. (A good starting point in this regard is to continue the Luke 15 passage. Sometimes new believers will experience a great deal of conflict with jealous "older brothers.")

Encourage everyone to offer at least one piece of advice or encouragement. In addition, have people indicate if they are willing to help your new believers get off to a good start—perhaps conducting Bible studies together, praying together, or simply sitting together in church. You might also, from an adult level, offer to do whatever you can to help the people get off to a good start as some of the newest members of God's kingdom.

Optional Extras

1. *Welcome Party.* Emphasize the "rejoicing" aspect of the shepherd, the woman, and the father, by throwing a party for some in the group who were dead and are alive again; who were lost and are found (see Luke 15:32). The bigger the celebration, the more important young people will come to feel that salvation is.

2. *Discipleship Group.* If you have had a number of new believers recently, you might consider starting a discipleship group geared especially for them. Perhaps you could even find a mature student volunteer to help lead it.

3. *Lost and Found.* Hide a treat (chocolate kisses or M & Ms) in the bottom of ice cream cones. Fill with ice cream and serve. Mention that you've hidden some other treats somewhere in the room, and have kids search for them while they eat their cones. If they find the treats before they finish their cones, they can have them. Your kids, however, will soon discover that the lost treats were literally under their noses the whole time!

Baptism

Baptism is an outward sign to signify the inner change that takes place in our lives when we put our trust in Jesus. It helps us identify ourselves with other believers.

Romans 6:1-14

Bibles
Pencils
Paper

1 *Shared Characteristics*

Note: This session refers primarily to believer's baptism. Do feel free to adapt it to represent your church's teaching on baptism.

Explain that you will name a series of characteristics. After each one, each person should find one other person who shares that particular characteristic with him or her. Anyone without a partner is eliminated.

Some of your characteristics might include: eye color, age, month of birth, length of hair, city of residence, school, favorite music group, number of brothers/sisters, shoe size, etc. Start with some of the categories that apply to most of the group members before you do some of the less common ones. From time to time, as the group dwindles, declare, "Everybody in," and start over with a different list of characteristics.

Later, refer to this activity to explain that baptism is a common bond for Christians. It is a sign of a shared experience—belief in Jesus.

2 **Find the Common Bond**

Have two people volunteer to play a game. One should be the clue-giver. The other should be the guesser. Give the first person a list of six categories. He or she should list items that are in that category until the other person can guess what the category is. See if the pair can guess all six categories in under a minute.

Some categories might include: things that float, red things, things with four legs, tennis items, parts of a shoe, things that jump, things that laugh, Arnold Schwarzenegger movies, Olympic athletes, famous sayings, biblical quotations, and so on. Within each list of six, try to include some of the harder categories along with the ones that may be a little more obvious. After one pair of volunteers has tried, let other pairs try (as time permits), using different lists of categories.

3 **Show Some I. D.**

Have group members take stock of anything they are wearing or carrying that might indicate an association with a specific group. Some will be more obvious than others, but even the more obscure things should be noted. Some such things might include: class rings, school sweatshirts, football jerseys, pins from organizations, library cards, school I. Ds., "going steady" rings, braided friendship bands, etc. Other things might include hairstyles, specific brand name clothing or shoes, and so forth. See how long a list your group can compile.

Ask: **When people look at us, how can they tell we belong to a group of Chris-**

tians? (Students may initially suggest outward indications: carrying Bibles, going to church, doing good things for others, Christian T-shirts or bumper stickers.)

Explain that becoming a Christian doesn't make us *look* any different, at least not physically. People might not tell that there has been a change within us. And going to church doesn't necessarily mean the individual has yielded his or her life to Jesus. That's why we have a way of publicly identifying with other Christians when we make that decision to put our faith in Him—baptism.

4 Examine the Purpose of Baptism

Ask: **Can you think of any "memorable" baptisms in the Bible?** (Some kids might mention Jesus' baptism [Matthew 3:13-17] or the baptism of the Philippian jailer and his family [Acts 16:29-34].) Remind group members that God sent John *the Baptist* to prepare the way for Jesus' ministry. Even before Jesus started teaching, John was baptizing "with water for repentance" (Matthew 3:11). But he knew that Jesus would "baptize you with the Holy Spirit and with fire."

After Jesus' death and resurrection, baptism came to reflect a person's faith in His saving power. It was almost an immediate follow-up to the person's conversion. Through baptism, the person declared to the public that he or she was a Christian, a considerably more risky action in those days than it is now.

Have someone read Romans 6:1-10. Discuss:

• **What past event does baptism represent?** (It reminds us that Jesus died for us, and allows us to be buried with Him, in a sense—we experience a "death" to our old way of life. We were once bound by our sins, but that is behind us now.)

• **What future event does baptism represent?** (Since we share in the death of Jesus, we will also share in His resurrection. Though we haven't been physically resurrected yet, baptism symbolizes the fact that we *will* be.)

• **How is baptism significant for the present?** (Even though our "death" and "resurrection" are symbolic, we should begin to live for Jesus. Our behavior, thoughts, and attitudes should reflect our new life.)

• **Death isn't a very pleasant thing to think about. Why is that image so important in regard to baptism?** (Dead people don't have the ability to do much—including the ability to sin. We should consider ourselves alive only in the sense of serving Jesus. We have been freed from sin, but we must learn to live accordingly.)

Have someone read Romans 6:11-14. Discuss:

• **What are some ways that people "let sin reign" in their lives?** (Everyone is tempted by certain sins. Some give in easily to sin, and consequently, become slaves to the sin that results. Have group members provide specific examples, such as sexual activity or rage toward parents.)

• **What are some ways that people "offer the parts of their bodies to sin"?** (Again let students provide specific examples. For instance: eyes that regularly peruse pornography, ears eager for gossip, feet that take us places we shouldn't be, hands that shoplift items.)

• In each of the previous cases, how might we "offer ourselves to God" instead? (The eyes might be reading His Word, the ears could be listening to the needs of others, the feet could be taking us on service projects, the hands could be clasped in prayer, etc.)

5 Commit to Closeness

Summarize: **A credit card company recently ran an ad with the slogan, "Membership has its privileges." The slogan is true of the church as well. Baptism shows that we have put our faith in Jesus, which entitles us to certain privileges. What are some of them?**

Let kids respond as you compile a master list. Possible answers: a personal relationship with God, answered prayer, the right to be co-heirs with Christ, unity with other believers, the presence of the Holy Spirit in our lives, and so forth.

Explain that these are the results of salvation and baptism. However, sometimes we don't try very hard to claim the benefits that are rightfully ours. Ask each person to consider what he or she might need to do during the next few weeks to better identify with the death and resurrection of Jesus—or to identify with each other more closely. If volunteers are willing, let them share their goals. Conclude with sentence prayers to let individuals thank God for their new life.

Optional Extras

1. *Water Fun.* Plan a swim party, a trip to a water park, or some other water-oriented fun activity to celebrate the recent baptism(s) in your group.

2. *Pastor's Input.* Invite your pastor to be present at this session to deal with baptism on a more doctrinal level and to answer any questions your group members might have.

Group Closeness

BIG IDEA

All growing youth groups are marked by a healthy sense of unity—sharing experiences and building up one another.

BIBLE INPUT

John 17:20-23
Romans 15:1-7
Ephesians 4:1-6, 25-32
Colossians 3:12-17

BRING:

Bibles
Pencils
Paper
A ball of yarn

1 Play Anatomy

Have everyone get a partner. Form two groups with one person from each pair in each group. One group should form a large circle, and the other group should form a smaller circle within the first one. Begin with partners facing each other. Then the inner circle should begin to rotate clockwise as the outer circle rotates counter-clockwise. At random intervals, call out two body parts, such as, "Right knee to left elbow." Immediately partners should find each other and attach the *inner circle person's* right knee to the *outer circle person's* left elbow. The last pair to do so is eliminated. Then circles are reestablished and put back into motion until you call out another pair of anatomical parts. (Be creative!) When only two pairs remain, a "Nose to right armpit" command usually determines which group members are really playing to win.

2 Sniff Out Your Shoes

Have everyone sit on the floor in a circle, remove their shoes, and place them in the center of the circle. Have everyone close their eyes as you mix the shoes well. Then, with all eyes still closed tightly, each person tries to locate his or her own pair of shoes. The first person to find *and put on* both shoes is the winner.

3 Create Closeness Analogies

Say: **It takes a close group to participate in those two activities. But there is more to group closeness than body parts and shoes.** Pull out a ball of yarn as you ask kids to create some analogies that apply to your group. The formula they may want to use is: **Our group is like a _____ because _____.**

Give some examples, such as, **Our group is like a mosaic, because when every "tile" is in place, we're a classic work of art.** Or, **I think our group is like a herd of animals because we're a little bit on the wild side, but willing to gather around and try to protect each other when faced with danger.** Or, of course, the biblical example is: **Our group is like a body because each person has a specific ability, and when we work together we become complete and effective.**

Have everyone think of at least one example, more if they can. These need not be profound. Most are likely to reflect the personalities of your kids, whether humorous, simple, athletic, or whatever. After you give an example or two, hold the end of the yarn and toss the ball on to another person who should share an analogy, wrap the yarn around a wrist or finger, and toss the ball of yarn to another person. (The more of a tangle you create, the better.)

After most of the analogies have been exhausted, say: **Right now we're all bonded together with this yarn. But we can't always count on being literally united. What is it that bonds us on a more permanent basis?** (Let kids respond. Perhaps they will find more than one correct answer, such as "The love of God," and "The Holy Spirit in our lives." If this happens, let them continue the discussion until they make clear the connection between the two.)

4 Establish and Maintain Unity

Explain that unity should be a goal of any Christian group. While the current strength of the group is a reason to celebrate, group closeness is not something to take for granted. It needs continual attention on the part of each individual. It is counterproductive to bicker, fight, or gossip and ask God to bless us. While He supplies us with abundant love and with the power of the Holy Spirit, we must choose to submit to His leading as He draws us closer to others.

Have someone read John 17:20-23. Explain that these verses are part of a prayer Jesus prayed just before He was arrested and crucified. His desire for His followers was "complete unity." Break into four groups (even if it's a one-person group) and assign each group one of the following passages to read and report on. Groups should look for instructions regarding unity, and come up with a number of observations. Also challenge them to come up with some specific examples from their own lives. Bring out these points in your discussion.

Romans 15:1-7. Unity depends on those who are spiritually strong "bearing with" less mature people. We should follow Jesus' example who came to serve others. When we need endurance and encouragement, God provides it for us.

Ephesians 4:1-6. We should exhibit humility, gentleness, and patience. God's love is a wonderful gift we have received. It's not something we can earn or deserve, though we should "live a life worthy of" His love. Unity is possible when we "make every effort." As each person draws closer to God, we all draw closer to each other as well.

Ephesians 4:25-32. Lying and anger are quick to destroy unity. We must learn to be truthful, and to get angry without sinning. Even little things we say and do can have destructive effects, so we need to get rid of *all* unwholesome talk, bitterness, rage, anger, brawling, slander, and other negative behaviors. Instead of retaliating when others offend us, we need to be kind, compassionate, and forgiving.

Colossians 3:12-17. The key to practicing compassion, kindness, humility, gentleness, and patience is love. God's love helps us to bear with one another and forgive each other. As we do, we can experience peace. God's Word guides us, and we should respond with songs of gratitude. Everything we do should be done in recognition of God's involvement in our lives and with thankfulness to Him.

5 Remember to Respond

No group goes from being selfish to being unified overnight. Even a group which is especially close can use some improvement. Have every person think of one specific area from these passages (or another portion of Scripture) that he or she could improve in, and then share his or her goal for unity with the group.

Perhaps someone feels she is doing all she can to get along with others, yet has not felt the peace that is promised. She might say, "I am going to try to experience God's peace during the next few weeks." Someone may have strong friendships with peers, yet a rocky relationship with his parents. He should express his intention to demonstrate a more loving attitude toward Mom and Dad. As soon as each person shares an area to work on, tie a piece of yarn around his or her finger as a reminder. Encourage everyone to wear the reminder home and then place the yarn somewhere it will be seen on a regular basis (taped to a mirror, a bookmark, etc.).

Close with a prayer thanking God for the unity that exists, and asking Him for an even greater sense of group closeness in the months to come.

Optional Extras

1. *Value Diversity.* Even if your group is close, they're still individuals. To show this, create a number of opinion questions for kids to answer. Read the answers aloud to show the differing opinions. Unity doesn't mean becoming clones, but learning to appreciate each other's differences.

2. *Unity Candle in Reverse.* Ask kids if they've ever seen a unity candle at a wedding. If so, have them describe it. (The bride and groom use separate candles to light one new, common candle; then they blow out the individual ones.) To symbolize your unity in Christ, start with one candle. Give each kid a separate candle and light each one from the common flame. This will be more effective in a darkened room. Sing a song such as "Shine, Jesus, Shine" or "They'll Know We Are Christians" as you light the candles. Place the candles through squares of wax paper to prevent wax burns!

Numerical Growth

BIG IDEA

A growing group gives us cause to celebrate and motivates us to keep reaching out.

BIBLE INPUT

Acts 1:15; 2:41; 4:4; 4:32—5:11; 6:7

BRING:

Bibles
Calculator

1 Play Sheep and Wolves

Note: If your group hasn't grown in size, this session could be used to motivate your group to reach out more.

Have everyone gather on one side of the room or lawn (if you're playing outside) except for one person in the center, designated as the wolf. The goal of the sheep is to race to the opposite side without getting tagged. When a sheep has been tagged three times, it becomes a wolf and joins the original wolf in trying to tag the other sheep. The three tags don't have to come from the same wolf, but the same wolf can't tag a sheep more than once on each pass. Keep count of the passes and see how long it takes for all the sheep to become wolves. (Later explain that the purpose of your group is to reverse the sheep-to-wolves process. You want a safe environment for God's sheep, perhaps converting a few "wolves" along the way.)

2 Complete Sentences

Begin a number of sentences and let group members verbally express their thoughts regarding the size of your group. For example:
- I think the ideal size for our group would be . . .
- If our group were larger, we could . . .
- The problems with having a larger group would be . . .
- One thing I liked when we were smaller was . . .
- If we *really* wanted this group to grow, we should . . .
- You can tell a group is getting too big when . . .
- Some things are even more important than the size of the group, like . . .

3 Compare Growth Strategies

Suppose you stop to help a guy change a tire, and when you finish he tells you he is a billionaire. He says, "Because you helped me, you have restored my faith in young people and I want to reward you. I'll give you a choice. Choice one is that I hand you one million dollars cash on the spot. Choice two is that I'll give you a penny instead. But tomorrow I'll give you two cents. The day after tomorrow I'll give you four cents. I'll double the amount every day for 30 days. Take a few moments to decide, and then tell me which you would prefer."

Provide a calculator and let students make a few calculations. If they get as far as Day 15, they'll see that they will have accumulated only $327.67. At about that point, ask them to decide. Let them indicate by show of hands whether they would select Choice 1 (the even million dollars) or Choice 2. While that first little penny might not seem like much compared to a million-dollar pile of cash, if it is doubled 30 times, the grand total at the end of 30 days is $10,737,418.23. Kids who made Choice 2 and waited patiently would come out more than ten times better.

Compare this exercise to the numerical growth of your group. Too often we count on a major event to bring people in. But more effective is each person inviting his or her friends. It might take time to grow, but the end result is worth it. Remind everyone that growth should be an ongoing goal. And it is *everyone's* responsibility to spread the word about what goes on at your meetings.

4 Growth Spurt for the Church

Ask: **How many Christians do you think there are in the world today?** (Let kids speculate.) **How many were there to begin with?** (Initially, only Jesus' disciples and a few other followers knew the truth about who Jesus was and why He had come.) **How did the number of believers grow from such a small number to such a large one?** (Kids may tend to focus on activities such as preaching and evangelism, which are correct responses. In addition to these specific activities was a group of believers who put the Gospel into practice. Not everyone has the gift of a pastor or evangelist, but everyone can show God's love.)

Trace the growth of the early church by having volunteers read:

- Acts 1:15 (where believers numbered about 120)
- Acts 2:41 (where 3,000 more were added in one day)
- Acts 4:4 (where the total of men was up to 5,000)
- Acts 6:7 (which indicates that the growth was rapid and continual).

Explain that the Holy Spirit was moving people to respond to the message during this time, which accounts for the significant advancement of the Gospel. Ask: **Do you think these people were hearing sermons and instantly changing their life-styles, or do you think other things were going on as well?** (Let kids respond. See if they are aware that the actions of the believers during this time backed up the message that was being preached.)

Have a volunteer read Acts 4:32-35. As he or she does, have the rest of the group members listen for the things that were going on that might have attracted others to Christianity. Their list should include:

- A spirit of unity
- The personal testimony of the apostles
- God's power and grace (seeing God at work among them)
- The sharing and selling of possessions to meet the needs of others.

Discuss: **As others see what's going on in our group, how well do you think we would rate in each of these areas? Explain.** Let group members evaluate each area.

Then ask: **If we are doing these things and attracting new people, do you think that would guarantee God's blessing on us as a group and as individuals?** Let group members respond, and then have someone read Acts 4:36—5:11. Discuss:

- **What was the main difference between Barnabas and Ananias and**

Sapphira? (Barnabas gave wholeheartedly. Ananias and Sapphira held back some of what they had made from the sale of their property.)

• **Didn't Ananias and Sapphira have the right to keep part of the money?** (Sure, but their sin was in trying to make it appear that they had given all.)

• **What exactly was it that they did wrong?** (Peter accused them of "lying to the Holy Spirit." They lied to make themselves look better than anyone else.)

• **Do you think their punishment was a bit severe? Why do you think God dealt with them so strongly?** (This was the very beginning of the church. If others discovered what Ananias and Sapphira had done, the integrity of the church as well as the power of God might have been brought into question. God showed His people that He was serious about developing qualities such as honesty and trust.)

5 Choose a Growth Goal

Have each group member think of one specific area that he or she needs to develop in order to help the group continue to grow. It might be interactive, such as witnessing, fellowship, or service. Or it might be more personal: prayer, Bible study, or increased patience. After group members determine *what* they need to do, have them also think specifically *how* they can get started this week.

Optional Extras

1. *Service Project.* Plan a service project, such as a group garage sale, where the work (or the proceeds) can be devoted to a worthy cause in your church or neighborhood.

2. *Painting by Numbers.* Attach a large sheet of paper to your wall. Give one group member a marker and have him or her draw one line on the paper. The next member can draw two more lines, the next member four, and soon. After five or six rounds, your mural should be quite impressive. If you have a large group, you many need to create several murals at once.

Spiritual Growth

BIG IDEA — While numerical growth is easier to recognize, a better indication of a group's effectiveness and faithfulness to God is continual spiritual maturity among its individual members.

BIBLE INPUT — I Corinthians 1:18-31; 3:1-3

BRING: Bibles
Pencils
Paper
Baby food (If possible, one jar for every two people)

1 Race to Get in Order

Divide into teams with an equal number of people on each team (six to ten per team is ideal). Explain that you will announce a category, such as "alphabetical order based on your last name." Each team should then try to line up from A to Z, as quickly as possible. Include a lot of growth comparisons (height, hair length, shoe size, age, size of hand span, length of leg, etc.) Avoid any potentially embarrassing comparisons such as weight, waist size, and so on.

2 Graph Physical Growth

Hand out pens and paper and have each person draw a not necessarily realistic graph of his or her physical growth. Along the bottom they should draw a time line from "Birth" at the left to "Now" on the right. Along the left side, they need to draw a height scale going from zero feet at the bottom to seven feet at the top. Group members may creatively plot out growth spurts or slow times till they reached their present heights.

When everyone finishes, collect the graphs and mix them up. Give the current height of the first person, show the graph, and see how well everyone can guess whose it is. Then go through the rest of them (quickly).

3 Spiritual Nourishment

Say: **For most of us, growing, at least height-wise, takes place on its own. We don't have to work too hard to go from nineteen inches at birth to five-feet-some-odd inches by now. However, spiritual growth is another matter. What are some ways that you can tell whether you or someone else is growing spiritually?**

As group members brainstorm *specific* ways to evaluate spiritual growth, write down their responses. The list may include things such as regular times of Bible study and prayer, fellowship with other Christians, church attendance, missions involvement, and giving. Challenge them to think in terms of spiritual maturity on a personal level, such as "turning the other cheek" when offended, submitting to someone else to avoid an unnecessary argument, not carrying grudges, etc.

After you compile a list, hand out jars of baby food. (Use a couple of volunteers if you have only one jar, but the more jars you have, the better.) Designate one person in each pair as the feeder and the other as the "feedee." Explain that the feeder is to feed his or her partner specially prepared spiritual food you have brought. Then use the list you just made as a basis for questions such as these:

• **During the previous week, have you told anyone outside this group that** you're a Christian? (If not, have feeder provide person with some "spiritual" food.)

• **Have you read the Bible each day this week?** (One spoonful [or fingertip] of food for each day missed.)

• **Have you prayed every day this week?**

• **Can you remember the topic of the pastor's sermon this week?**

• **Do you remember what we talked about in this group last week?**

• **Are you holding any grudges right now?** (Perhaps toward the feeder?)

• **Have you had an argument with your parents this week that could have been avoided?**

In each case, the feeders should to determine how many spoonfuls of food the feedees need to become as mature as they feel necessary. If feeders become a little too smug in their responsibilities along the way, suddenly switch roles.

Explain the significance of this activity by having someone read I Corinthians 3:1-3. Point out that Paul, as a teacher of the Corinthians, wanted to deal with some of the "meatier" parts of Scripture, but they were not grown up enough spiritually to handle it. Therefore, Paul had to stick to "baby food."

4 Learn Which Goal to Seek

What are some reasons that spiritual growth is so hard? (It requires a commitment of time and priority. With all the activities of life, it's easy to let spiritual disciplines slide. Also, spiritual maturity demands that we set aside some goals the rest of the world has in order to follow God's will.)

When Christians continue to interact but not grow spiritually, what is likely to happen? (It's only a matter of time until human nature takes over, and they begin to become selfish, argumentative, jealous, and so on.)

Explain that this was the case in Corinth when Paul wrote I Corinthians. **The Christians were arguing over unimportant issues (1:10-12) and had stagnated in their spiritual growth (3:1-3). As Paul opened his letter, he wanted them to realize what their goal should be.**

Have someone read I Corinthians 1:18-31. Then discuss:

• **Have you ever been embarrassed or a little uncomfortable when you tried to explain Christianity to someone? If so, why?** (Jesus' sacrifice on the cross is not logical to most people hearing it for the first time. It sounds like "foolishness.")

• **If God knew that the Gospel message would sound so weird to people, why didn't He do something more "logical" instead?** (For one thing, believing something out of the ordinary requires faith. But even more significantly, as we begin to understand God's plan of salvation and to grow, it begins to make sense.)

• **How does the message of the Gospel affect one's relationship with God?** (Although it requires His wisdom to understand it, we can realize our inability to save ourselves and turn to God in faith. People who try to achieve salvation on their own will be frustrated because no one is "good" enough to deserve it.)

• **How do you feel when Paul says that God chose the "foolish," "weak,"** "lowly," and "despised" things to accomplish His purposes? (Spiritual maturity includes recognizing that these adjectives are true of us—at least before God enters our lives.)

• **Do you tend to boast more about yourself or about God? Explain.** (Most people tend to take pride in the things they can do. But in time, we should learn to take pride in the things which God empowers us to do. The accomplishments may be the same, but the perspective is entirely different.)

5 Graph Spiritual Growth

Have group members make another graph similar to the one in Step 2, but this time have them chart the progress they have made spiritually. They should indicate when they chose to believe in Jesus, and how they have grown (or stayed the same) since then. Be sensitive to those who may not be Christians yet. Also ask kids to leave some room on the right side of the graph to do a "projection" of spiritual growth. If they are satisfied with their current progress, perhaps they want to see the same rate of growth. If not, they may want to see a sharper upward rise.

When they finish, let volunteers explain their graphs. After a few have done so, encourage your kids to keep growing spiritually. No one can hold steady. Either we are getting closer to God, or falling away from Him. Close with a prayer, thanking God for all He has done and for His help as you all continue to grow.

Optional Extras

1. *Growth Groups.* If group members are indeed growing spiritually, you might want to consider starting some new small groups (More intensive Bible study? Discipleship? Evangelism?) for anyone who is interested.

2. *Testimonies.* If some group members seem resistant to spiritual maturity, ask some of the adults in your church to give testimonies to the young people, describing the difficulties of their youth and their subsequent growth.

Completed Service Project

BIG IDEA

As we celebrate how good we feel after serving others, we also want to maintain a humble spirit and not get too proud of our own accomplishments.

BIBLE INPUT

I Corinthians 2:1-5; 3:5-9

BRING:

Bibles
Pencils
Stationery

1 Designate a King or Queen

As you begin your meeting, select one person to be king (or queen). This person should have special privileges during any activity. For example, if you are running relays, the king can have another team member run in his place (if he so chooses). If each person is usually responsible for getting his or her own chair, cleaning up after himself, or whatever, the king can assign someone to do the job for him.

Watch for a while and see what kind of "ruler" your king or queen turns out to be. If he abuses his newfound power, revoke his privileges and make someone else king (preferably someone who suffered at the hands of the former king). Perhaps your group members will discover that "whoever wants to become great among you must be your servant" (Matthew 20:26).

2 Conduct an Excuse-a-thon

Have group members sit in a circle. Suggest an opportunity for service, real or imaginary, and have each person give an excuse to avoid participating. Anyone who cannot think of a different excuse is eliminated. Keep going until you see who is best at coming up with reasons not to do something. Any excuse that has not been used previously should be accepted.

Point out that if people don't want to do something, there are always a multitude of reasons they can give. Genuine service requires a willingness to leave the excuses behind and get to work on someone else's behalf.

3 Share Lessons Learned

Although service projects are usually designed to help others in some way, they usually provide a lot of insight and personal growth for the participants as well. Let those who took part in the service project explain to the others what they learned. You might want to guide the discussion around some main themes:
- Discoveries about the person(s) being helped
- Discoveries about others in the group
- Discoveries about God
- Discoveries about oneself

Some people may be a bit hesitant to speak up at first, but after the bolder ones break the ice, it may be surprising to hear the depth of discovery some of the quieter ones gleaned from their recent experience. (You should be sure to respond as well. When young people see that adults continue to discover new things, they are more likely to perceive service and spiritual growth as long-term endeavors.)

The Importance of Follow-up

Say something to the effect of: **When it comes to serving others, the apostle Paul is a pretty good role model. After his dramatic conversion to Christianity, Paul devoted his life to on-the-road service. He preached, built up the young churches, and provided guidance and insight—all the while sacrificing his own personal comfort to do so. One of the most impressive things about Paul was that he didn't simply move from one place to another, leaving his previous ministries and relationships in the dust. He truly cared about and regularly prayed for the places he had already been as well as the people at his new assignment. One example is found in his first letter to the Corinthian church, which was a follow-up to his previous visit there.**

Have someone read I Corinthians 2:1-5. Discuss:

• **Do you share any of Paul's feelings? If so, which ones?** (Perhaps the weakness, fear, and trembling beforehand. Or some may relate to a lack of eloquence.)

• **If Paul was so fearful, why did he put himself to all the trouble?** (He realized that he wasn't expected to know it all. He was satisfied to share what he *did* know about Jesus with others.)

• **How did Paul overcome his initial anxiety?** (He trusted God to provide power from the Holy Spirit.)

• **What was the result of Paul's efforts?** (The Corinthians didn't believe Paul because of his fancy talk, but because they could see that God was working in his life. Consequently, God got the glory instead of Paul—as it should be.)

Continue: **However, since Paul's visit, the Corinthians had come into contact with other spiritual leaders, such as Apollos. Perhaps Apollos was a more entertaining speaker than Paul. Whatever the reason, the church members had become split in their loyalties. Some thought Paul was still the greatest. Some liked Apollos better. Some had other favorites.**

Have someone read I Corinthians 3:5-9, and then discuss:

• **What did Paul think about his loyal "fan club"?** (He reprimanded the Corinthians for divisions in the church based on the personalities of their leaders.)

• **What was the big problem with people getting excited about what Paul was saying?** (The Corinthians were getting caught up by the speakers rather than focusing on the message. Paul reminded them that both he and Apollos were only servants who represented God. Two people who minister in the same place should build on each other rather than divide the church.)

• **In light of our recent service project, what can we learn from Paul's words to the Corinthians?** (We honor God with our acts of service, even if those we serve don't respond exactly the way we had hoped; we should remember to give God the glory for any positive results; we shouldn't compare the results of our service project with anyone else's, either for better or worse, because all actions are equally important to God; and we do well to follow up on our acts of service to ensure that the people served know that they won't be quickly forgotten.)

5 A Special Follow-up to Service

Just as Paul followed up his visit to the Corinthians with a letter (actually, more than one letter), encourage your group members to think of an appropriate way to follow up their service project. If they helped build or repair homes and established some relationships with the people there, they could call or write. If they had some kind of public evangelistic project, it might be difficult for personal contact; however, there may be hosts to thank. Perhaps they can thank anyone in the church who supported the project. Such people are truly partners in ministry.

Provide stationery so group members can write as many people as is appropriate. If many people need to be written, let each person write one or more letters. If only a few, divide into groups and make sure everyone contributes to at least one letter (or call). Make this as pleasurable as possible. If follow-up seems a chore in this case, group members may be reluctant to try again next time. Close with a prayer for the specific needs of the person(s) you served.

Optional Extras

1. *World Missions.* Contact some missions agencies and ask them to provide your group with information about their ministries. After group members experience the needs of one person or group on a firsthand basis, the other ministries around the world are likely to become more real to them.

2. *Table Service.* Put an assortment of objects that could be used to serve others (work gloves, money, a rake, etc.) on a table. Try to have at least twenty items. Cover the stuff with a tablecloth. Remove the cloth and let kids study the items for about one minute. Cover the items and have kids write down what they remember seeing on the table. As kids call out the items, have them share one way these items could be used to serve others.

Good-bye to Group Member

BIG IDEA

Christians never say good-bye forever. One day we will have a magnificent reunion that will never end.

BIBLE INPUT

Philippians 1:3-11

BRING:

Bibles
Pencils
Paper
Camera with film

1 *Group Photographers*

Note: You might want to use this session at the end of your year together.
Throughout this session, let two people drop out of the activities from time to time to take pictures. Show them how to use the camera and tell them to capture a pictorial account of the departing group member's last meeting. (They should alternate the picture-taking responsibilities so both will be included in the shots when the film is developed.) Make sure they ration the supply of film so there will be plenty for group shots at the end of the session.

2 *Impersonations*

Say something to the effect of: **When Elvis said good-bye to this world he spawned a hoard of people whose sole ambition in life was imitating him until they died. Therefore, in a way, he would continue to live. But Elvis wasn't any more important than** (name of departing person) **is. So take a couple of minutes to rehearse and see how well you can impersonate _____.**

Explain that these impersonations need not be long—perhaps just a phrase or two. Have some fun with this. Maintain the sense that this is a tribute to the person, and not a mockery. (If your group has difficulty impersonating the person, have them share thoughts or recall stories about him or her instead.)

3 *A Thousand Good-byes*

Hand out pencils and paper and have each person make a list of ways to say good-bye. Explain that they should try to go beyond some of the more obvious methods. In fact, if two people write down the same thing, neither person will get credit for it.

After a few minutes of personal brainstorming time, have someone read one of his or her responses. Others who have that response should mark it off their lists. Then move to the next person, and on around until you get to the responses that are not so common.

Any response that indicates a form of saying good-bye should be allowed. Some might be words: *farewell, see you later, adios, sayanara,* and so forth. In a letter, people sign off with "Yours truly," "Sincerely," or some other closing. A husband says good-bye to his wife with a hug or a kiss. Vikings said good-bye to their dead warriors by placing them on a flaming ship and floating them out to sea. Any of these responses should be accepted. Where appropriate, have students say or do them to your departing group member.

4 *The Bright Side of Good-bye*

Say: **Right now, most of you are unable to feel glad, but there are reasons you all should be able to celebrate later. While saying good-bye is never easy, Christians never say good-bye to each other forever.**

Have everyone find Philippians 1:3-11 and do a verse-by-verse study to discover reasons to celebrate departing from good friends. Your kids might discover:

• Verse 3—Memories of each other are to be treasured and should result in thanksgiving to God because of the other person(s).

• Verse 4—Memories of each other should lead to prayers on behalf of the other person(s), and prayer leads to joy. (If we get all depressed and mopey, we're probably not talking to God as we should.)

• Verse 5—We continue to be partners in the work of God even after the person moves away. Whether we work side by side or on opposite sides of the world, Christians are working together for the same purposes—personal spiritual growth and the spread of the knowledge of Jesus to others.

• Verse 6—In fact, as God continues to work in all of us, the best is yet to come. Note also that there *will* be a "day of Christ Jesus." We as Christians will all be united again, whether or not we ever see each other again here on earth.

• Verse 7—We have the person in our hearts, and we will be in his (or hers). We continue to share in God's grace (favor that we don't deserve). God brought us together in this fellowship, and wherever we go from now on we will be better people because of it.

• Verse 8—We will certainly miss each other, but in a very special way. As we experience the love of Christ in our lives, we spread it to other people. So rather than the emptiness of separation, we should feel a bond of love that spans the distance between ourselves and the person(s) we care about.

• Verses 9-11—We aren't just saying, "Good-bye. Good luck. So long. We wish you the best." Rather, we will be praying:

(1) That love will increase for all of us, whether we stay or go

(2) For knowledge in insight to know where God will take us all from here

(3) For the ability to *know* what is best;

(4) For a pure and blameless Christian life (and another group of good Christian friends in the person's new surroundings);

(5) For the righteousness that only God can provide and

(6) That everything resulting from this separation will bring glory and praise to God.

Remind group members of how terrible the disciples must have felt after Jesus was crucified. Their despair must have been overwhelming. But Jesus reappeared to let them know that not even death is able to separate Christian friends. As a result, the disciples devoted their lives to telling others about Jesus, and Christianity spread throughout the world. If our focus remains on God's love and power rather than on our own sorrow, we will grow stronger through this experience.

5 *Surrounded with Love*

Before you say good-bye for the last time, surround the departing person with a group hug. Have everyone in the group hold hands in a continuous line standing side by side and facing the same way. The honoree should be on the end. He should then begin to "roll himself up" into the rest of the group (like a cinnamon roll, with the person ending up in the very center). Then, from the outside in, group members should exert gentle pressure toward the center.

Follow up with a prayer for the person leaving. Then close with some group pictures. Have two copies made of each set. Send one to the departing person and keep the second set for your own group.

Optional Extras

1. *Keep in Touch.* Have someone volunteer to be the "Official Correspondent" to the departing person for the next year. This person should be responsible to let the person know of the group's activities and to keep in touch. This person can also be the one designated to receive letters from the one leaving, so he or she doesn't have to write everyone.

2. *Bring New Friends.* Challenge group members to fill the hole in the group being left by the person leaving. If each person brings a new friend or classmate to the group, think what a difference it could make.

3. *Tug at Heartstrings.* To pack an emotional punch, play a recording of Michael W. Smith's song "Friends," right before your prayer time. Encourage kids to sing along.

Thanking Youth Sponsors

BIG IDEA

We shouldn't take for granted the spiritual leaders God has placed in our lives.

BIBLE INPUT

Numbers 13:26—14:10

BRING:

Bibles
Pencils
Paper

1 Take a Quiz

Have the youth sponsor(s) you are honoring supply a number of quiz questions about himself (or themselves), based on facts that a good friend might have discovered over the course of time (such as middle name, favorite musicians, extracurricular interests in high school/college, favorite sports teams, any allergies or physical limitations, and so forth). First read the list of questions and have kids record their answers. Then go back through the questions one at a time and have the youth sponsor(s) provide the correct answers, and discover which of the young people has gotten to know the youth sponsor(s) best (or are the best guessers).

2 List Reasons for Appreciation

Using the letters of each sponsor's name as a basis, have group members create reasons why they appreciate that person. For example, if the sponsor's name is Steve, a student might record that he is **S**haring, **T**ruthful, **E**nergetic, **V**ulnerable, and **E**ncouraging. Some of your more creative group members might try to form sentences where each word begins with the person's name. For example: STEVE– **S**hows **T**hankfulness **E**verywhere, **V**ery **E**nthusiastically. As group members try to fit this specific formula, they are likely to think of qualities of the person they are not able to use. So afterward, let them express all these things in addition to the qualities they already listed.

3 Now a Word from Your Sponsor

Let your youth sponsor(s) respond to what has been said. If the sponsors are so inclined, ask them to tell personal stories about events or experiences that taught them valuable lessons about God or about life. Young people relate well to the experiences of others, so sponsors should try to open up and be comfortable about sharing almost anything.

If your youth sponsors are more reserved, conduct a question-and-answer session instead. Have young people write out questions they would like to have the youth sponsors answer (about past relationships, opinions about debatable issues, etc.). Let someone act as emcee to collect the questions, interview the sponsor(s), and generate good discussion.

Servant Leadership

Explain that many times good youth sponsors are people who have been devoted to God for a number of years. Two biblical examples of this were Joshua and Caleb. Give some background on Moses' spy mission into the promised land (Numbers 13:1-25). Then have someone read Numbers 13:26–14:10. Skip over the strange-sounding names if you need to and remain focused on the action of the story. Discuss:

• **Joshua and Caleb saw the same things as all the other spies, so why was their report different?** (They had faith that God would help them overcome any obstacles.)

• **Specifically, why were the other ten spies so scared to enter Canaan?** (They were intimidated by the size and strength of the people who lived there.)

• **What were the people willing to give up rather than move forward in faith?** (Even after a miraculous deliverance from Egypt, they were now willing to give up bountiful land, great food, plenty of water, and even their very freedom. They were ready to become slaves again rather than trust God.)

• **How strongly did the people disagree with Joshua and Caleb?** (The people were ready to stone Joshua and Caleb, but God intervened.)

• **Who in this story do you most relate to? Explain.** (Moses and Aaron, the leaders who got little if any cooperation from the group? Joshua and Caleb, the faithful minority? The other ten spies who were unable to see things from God's perspective? The whiney Israelites who preferred to go back into slavery rather than take a risk in faith?)

• **Does anyone know what happened to Joshua, Caleb, and the Israelites after this incident?** (God had them wander in the wilderness for an additional forty years, where everyone twenty years old or older would die. The only exceptions were Joshua and Caleb. God still gave His people what He had promised, but He gave the land to another generation who had developed faith.)

• **Do you think it was fair that Joshua and Caleb had to wander through the wilderness just like everyone else?** (It may not seem so. But in one sense, they became "youth directors" who trained the new generation of Israelites. Then forty years later, when they were finally ready to enter the promised land with confidence in God, Joshua was their leader and Caleb received a prime piece of real estate for an inheritance [Joshua 14:6-1].)

Ask young people to share what they can learn from this story. (God empowers us to do things we can't do on our own; risk plus faith should be an element in spiritual development, and so forth.) In addition to all the other lessons learned, be sure to emphasize the importance of learning from older, more mature Christians. Youth sponsors who devote time, are models, and offer prayers for the group are to be appreciated.

5 A Time for Personal Thanks

Provide pens and paper for everyone and have each person write a note of thanks to the youth sponsor(s). Encourage kids to be as specific as possible in reasons why they appreciate their group leader(s). Then conclude with a prayer of thanksgiving for the person(s) and all he or she has provided for the youth group.

Optional Extras

1. *Do-it-yourself Cake.* Provide group members with sprinkles, icing, and materials to decorate cookies or cupcakes for the youth sponsor(s) being honored.

2. *Gratitude Gift.* Give the youth sponsors a gift of some kind as a token of your appreciation.

3. *Pastor Appreciation.* Follow up this event with a similar thank-you program for the pastor of your church.

Exam Break

BIG IDEA Whenever the stresses of life increase in intensity, so should our faith and our dependence on God.

BIBLE INPUT Matthew 6:25-34

BRING: Bibles
Pencils
Paper
Bag of balloons in
assorted sizes and
shapes

1 Create Characters

Note: This session is intended for use during exam week, when kids are feeling the pressure from their big tests. Keep it short, and make it as fun as possible.

Divide into groups and ask each group to create a character and a skit to show how people cope with stress (especially exams). For example, groups might come up with a Whitney Whiner, Xavier Excuse-Giver, Pricilla Procrastinator, Patti Panic, Blair Blamer, etc. One person in each group should personify the character, and the others should contribute to the skit in some way. Let each group present its skit. Then brainstorm any other "characters" who may not have been represented in the skits, but could have been.

2 Let Out That Pent-Up Tension

Conduct a series of exercises that will help group members loosen up a bit. You know what will work best with your group, but here are a few suggestions :

• Team Scream—Divide into groups and have each group in turn scream to accomplish a number of predetermined effects. Have an impartial judge on hand to determine who is loudest, longest, shrillest, most creative, and so forth.

• Nonverbal Volume Contest—This is similar to the team scream, except group members are not allowed to make any noise with their mouths—no yelling, whistling, humming, or similar sounds. Instead, they must use any other means of noisemaking they can think of: stomping their feet, clapping, or whatever.

• Relays—Choose some of your favorite relays, the more active the better. Do a lot, so students can have some level of aerobic exercise.

• Play Ha!—Have group members lie on the ground with each person's head on the stomach of someone else. Begin at one end with each person in turn saying "Ha." When it gets to the end of the line, the process is reversed, with the end person saying "Ha Ha" and passing it back up the line. Keep adding a ha and see how far the group can get before becoming lost in infectious laughter.

3 Identify Group Stresses

Dump out an assortment of balloons and markers. Have students choose balloons, and blow them up; then use the markers to label each balloon with a specific source of stress. Say: **The bigger you blow up the balloon, the greater the pressure you feel.** Some balloons might represent tests, teachers, relationships, jobs, or parents. Explain that sometimes during major events like exams, other stresses of life seem to intensify.

When kids have finished, have them sit in a circle and throw the balloon the center. When the balloons have begun to pile up, move on to the Bible study.

4 Don't Worry, Be Faithful

Discuss:

• **On a scale of one to ten, how worried do you feel right now?** (Let kids answer with a "show of fingers.")

• **Can you be very worried about one thing, yet still function as usual?** (Most people can't. Serious worries affect almost everything else.)

• **When you find you are worried about something, let's say an exam, what are some ways that you cope with that anxiety?** (Have kids list as many things as they can think of. Some will probably be positive responses, such as prayer, studying harder, asking for help from parents or friends, and so forth. Many group members are likely to relate to nonproductive responses to worry: incapacitating fear, overeating, finding other worried people who tend to intensify the problem.)

• **Is worry always bad?** (It depends. Some see worry as a concern that can motivate them to action. Explain that the dictionary definition is "mental distress or agitation resulting from concern, usually for something impending or anticipated." When concern disintegrates into worry, it's counterproductive.)

Have someone read Matthew 6:25-30. Discuss:

• **What were the sources of worry mentioned in this passage?** (The references for what to eat, drink, and wear are rooted in concern for the basic needs of life. It's one thing to do poorly on an exam. It's completely another thing to not be sure where your next meal is going to come from.)

• **What purpose does worry serve?** (None. Worrying about a situation does absolutely nothing to solve it.)

• **When you see someone who worries a lot, what does that suggest about him or her?** (Probably the person may not really understand or believe that God has promised to look out for us.)

• **Does this mean that if you haven't studied all semester, and you count on God to help you, that you'll ace the exam?** (Not likely. However, trusting God to see you through the ordeal—no matter what happens—can help in a different way. God may not provide us with answers that we didn't bother to learn in the first place, but He can provide a sense of peace to help us recall what we *do* know.)

Have someone read Matthew 6:31-34. Discuss:

• **Rather than worrying, what should we do when faced with a stressful situation?** (We need to see things more from God's perspective. If we put His kingdom first, all the other things will fall in line.)

• **How does this apply to exam time?** (We don't have to take out our stress on other people. We can stay focused on God. We shouldn't panic, make excuses, procrastinate, or sidestep the issue. We need to draw on God's strength to see us through any situation and stop worrying so much.)

5 Stomp Out Worry

Have a period of silent prayer, during which individuals can express their worries to God. As you close the prayer, thank God for His constant provision for everyone, and ask for wisdom for the group members as they take the rest of their exams.

After the prayer, assume the demeanor of a coach doing a pregame pep-talk. Say something to the effect of: **OK. We're up against some tough opponents. Those worries are out there. Are we going to let them get us down? I can't *hear* you! Are we going to be defeated by these worries? I say you are tougher than those worries. I say you can stomp those worries. Are you with me?**

Conclude by having everyone literally stomp out the worries they listed by popping the balloons in the center of the circle. Then send the kids home to study.

Optional Extras

1. *Big Event.* Announce a post-exam big event that students can look forward to—something out of the ordinary like mud football, water balloon volleyball, or rent-a-gym night.

2. *This Is a Test.* Sometime during the session, give kids this silly test:

    1. Who's buried in Grant's Tomb? (Ulysses S. Grant)

    2. In what country were Venetian blinds invented? (Japan)

    3. In what town was the Woodstock Festival held? (Bethel, NY)

    4. How many gallons of water would it take to fill a ten-gallon hat? (about 3/4 of a gallon)

    5. Where were Panama hats first made? (Ecuador)

Have kids write down their answers before going over them. Award a prize to anyone who got one or more answers right.

DATE USED

School Year's End

BIG IDEA

We learn on an academic level because we're graded, or perhaps because we're forced or threatened. But on a spiritual level, we must choose to learn on a continuing basis.

BIBLE INPUT

Deuteronomy 5:1; 31:12
Isaiah 1:17
Matthew 11:28-30
John 14:28-31
I Thessalonians 4:3-8
I Timothy 5:4
Philippians 4:8-13

BRING:

Bibles
Pencils
Paper
Calendar

1 The Year's Best and Worst

Ask each group member to recall the one event of the previous school year that he or she remembers as the absolute best moment. Use the school calendar to bring to mind important events that have taken place. (The chosen event doesn't have to be connected with school, but should have occurred during the previous nine-month period.) If your group is not too large, have each person silently act out the event until the others guess what it was. In a large group, just let each person briefly describe it. Then go around again and have each person relate his or her worst memory of the past school year.

2 Compete in Pop Quizzes

Divide the group into two teams. Try to have an equal number of students on each team from every school represented in your group. Then ask each team to prepare a pop quiz for the other team, recalling facts learned during the school year. Any school subject is fair game. For example, the formula to compute the volume of a sphere; the dimensions of a volleyball court; etc. The key to preparing the quiz is that the team initiating the questions must know the correct answers. It is unfair to quiz the other team on subjects that students haven't taken. The point is for one team to recall more knowledge that the other team *should* have learned, but may not have retained. See if each group can develop ten questions.

After the quizzes are written, let the teams alternate asking questions. You can determine whether a question may be inappropriate (for example, if an honors physics student create the question and no one on the other team had the same class). But if the question is a fair one and the other team can't come up with the answer, award a point to the team that originated the question. Keep score for a while until a winner emerges. This exercise should reveal how much information that should be retained actually is forgotten as soon as there is no longer an accountability to know it. (Even creating the questions should give some indication of how well group members retain information.)

3 Grade Yourself

Explain that you will name a subject or category, and students should give themselves grades on how well they do in each category. Hand out pencils and paper so group members can create "flash card" grades to hold up so others can see. For example, you might say "History," and an average student would hold up a "C+" card while a good student would hold up an "A." After reading a few school subjects as categories, branch out into other things such as: friendship; truthfulness; family relationships; attitude toward authority; spiritual maturity; Bible knowledge; and so forth. Occasionally stop and have group members explain why they gave themselves a particular grade. Then discuss: **Do you usually devote more energy to the things where you receive tangible rewards such as grades or privileges? How much energy do you direct toward the things that make you a better person, yet don't have a lot of other tangible rewards?** (Have students provide specific examples.)

 # Learn about Learning

Ask: **How can you tell if you're a good student?** (See if group members think grades are accurate indicators of good students.) **Have you ever learned a lot in a class, yet didn't necessarily make a great grade? How do you gauge growth in areas like spiritual maturity where you don't get report cards?** (Let students respond.)

Explain that learning about God should be an ongoing goal for each of us, but sometimes it's difficult to keep up with because we have to be accountable on our own without written tests or grades. Yet we will surely face certain trials in life that will test what we know and believe to be true about God. Assign the following verses to individuals, pairs, or small groups. In each case the person(s) should describe what we should be learning in regard to our faith.

- Deuteronomy 5:1 (We should learn God's laws *and* follow them.)
- Deuteronomy 31:12 (We should learn to fear God [to have a deep reverence for Him].)
- Isaiah 1:17 (Learn to do right, seek justice, encourage the oppressed, defend the fatherless and widows.)
- Matthew 11:28-30 (Learn to find rest, gentleness, and humility from Jesus.)
- John 14:28-31 (Learn to understand Jesus' relationship with God the Father.)
- Philippians 4:8-13 (Learn to see positive qualities in other Christians and put them into practice in your own life as well.)
- I Thessalonians 4:3-8 (Learn to control our bodies in regard to sexual behavior, relationships with others, and living a holy life.)
- I Timothy 5:4 (Learn to act as good Christians to our own family members.)

Discuss: **If we're not getting graded on these things, why bother with them?** (We will be "graded" later. We will stand before God and give an account of our actions [Romans 14:9-12].) **Are you as concerned with learning these things as with your schoolwork?** (Let students respond.)

Schedule a Summer "Midterm"

Have each group member commit to doing one "homework" assignment from the previous list of verses or similar areas that might need attention, and have them write down what they are willing to do. Let those who are willing, share what they wrote: "I will volunteer to help in Vacation Bible School;" "I will try to stop arguing with Mom so often;" "I will devote more time to Bible study now that I'm out of school;" etc. Then collect the papers and select a date sometime in mid-summer. Explain that on that date, you will bring the papers you have just collected and have everyone grade themselves on the progress they are making. Then close in prayer, asking God to continue the spiritual "learning process" throughout the summer.

Optional Extras

1. *Teacher Appreciation Night.* Plan a Teacher Appreciation Night where you honor the schoolteachers in your church as well as Sunday School and special club leaders. Have students write letters of thanks for the training they have received from specific teachers.

2. *Summer Kickoff.* Schedule a picnic or cookout as a celebration of the end of the school year and the beginning of summer events.

3. *Textbook Games.* Bring in a bunch of old textbooks. Make up several games:
  • Who can balance the most books on his or her head?
  • Play tag or relay races, with each person balancing a book on his or her head. If the book falls, the person is out.
  • Line up several books across the room. Have kids pitch pennies, and award points for each penny that lands on top of a book.

Graduation

 **BIG IDEA**

While high school graduation is one of life's biggest highlights, the need for wisdom never ends.

 **BIBLE INPUT**

I Kings 3:5-15-28;
    4:29-34; 10:1-10,
14-29; 11:1-11

 **BRING:**

Bibles
Pencils
Paper
A trivia book or game

1 *Play a Trivia Game*

Using a book of trivia or a trivia game, design an elimination contest for group members. One option is to begin with everyone standing and ask each person a question. If the person answers correctly, he remains standing. If not, he sits down. Continue until only one person is standing.

Make a big deal about how this person must be the absolutely smartest person in the group—perhaps in the county. As you shower this person with praise, observe the others' responses and their comments. They are likely to point out that the knowledge of a few bits of trivia doesn't necessarily point to superior wisdom or intellect. If so, try to keep the conversation going in this direction. Ask: **Well, then, what *does* constitute wisdom? If you don't agree with the results of my little quiz, what do you think is a valid test to determine who is or isn't a wise person? Is there a difference between wisdom and intelligence?**

2 *Rate the Highlights of Life*

Explain that you want group members to rate a number of life events, indicating their responses by a "show of fingers." On a scale of one to ten (one being not important at all, and ten being very important), have them hold up the number of fingers that indicates their responses. Everyone should do this simultaneously, and keep holding up their fingers so everyone else can see the "ratings."

Some of the things to evaluate might include:
• Eighth grade graduation
• High school graduation
• College graduation
• Getting a job after college
• Changing jobs to get one you like better, at twice the salary
• Getting married
• Having a baby and a loving family of your own

Though right now, high school graduation might seem like the biggest possible event in a person's life, try to show through this exercise that even better things lie ahead. We need to perceive life as a series of "graduations." When we are children, most important life events are planned and scheduled for us. Later, however, the challenge we face is getting the most out of life on our own. As graduates leave the usually predictable world of high school, they must take the initiative in being responsible for their own lives.

3 Make a Wish

Ask: **If you could make a wish and be changed in any way, or receive anything you ask for, what would be your wish?** Make it clear that no limits exist on the extent of the wish. *Anything* is possible. Let each person respond in turn. Then briefly discuss the nature of the wishes.

There's a saying that we should be careful what we wish for, or we just might get it. The following Bible study on the life of Solomon shows that you better *use* what you wish for, or it really doesn't do you any good.

4 Review the Life of Solomon

Divide into five groups, and give each group an assignment to read about and report on one element of Solomon's life. The assignments for each group and highlights of each segment are listed below.

I Kings 3:5-15
As Solomon was just beginning his reign as king, God appeared to him in a dream, promising to give him anything he requested. Solomon asked for "a discerning heart to govern your people and to distinguish between right and wrong." Because of this unselfish request, God granted it, and added great riches and honor as well. The one thing God asked of Solomon was that "you walk in my ways and obey my statutes and commands."

I Kings 3:16-28
In an early test of Solomon's wisdom, two women wanted him to rule on who should have custody of a child both claimed as theirs. Solomon's decree to have the baby cut in half quickly showed the love of the real mother and the lack of genuine concern on the part of the impostor.

I Kings 4:29-34
Solomon wasn't just smart; he was brilliant. He spoke 3,000 proverbs and wrote 1,005 songs. People everywhere heard about him and traveled long distances to hear him. He knew about all sorts of things, including plant life, animals, birds, reptiles, fish, and so forth.

I Kings 10:1-10
One of the people who traveled to hear Solomon was the Queen of Sheba. She had a list of hard questions for him, and he answered them all. She was awestruck by the splendor and contentment of his kingdom and gave him lots of gifts.

I Kings 10:14-29

In addition to being the wisest person around, Solomon was also the richest. He had gold, ivory, ships, and chariots unlike anything people had ever seen. And silver was so common that it was not even considered valuable.

Ask: **With all this wealth, wisdom, and attention, what more could anyone ask for?** Let students respond. Then explain that it seems that Solomon was a straight A student when it came to life. However, he made an F on the final.

Have someone read I Kings 11:1-11. Discuss Solomon's downfall, and point out that wisdom is no good unless you *use* it. No matter what level of wisdom and resources we have, whether a little or a lot, we need to devote them to God. No amount will ever replace the need to have a good relationship with Him.

5 Create a Send-off for Graduates

Place all your graduates in one group. Let them talk among themselves about their plans for the future, and commit to remember to pray for one another. Meanwhile, have the other group members divide into teams, pairs, or individuals to come up with some kind of special recognition for the graduates (a card, song, skit, poem, "remembrance" card with names/addresses/phone numbers, etc.). After each person or group has performed or presented its tribute to the graduates, close in a prayer for wisdom for both those who will be moving on to new adventures as well as those who will be in the group for yet another year.

Optional Extras

1. *Postcard Packets.* Bring some postcards to the meeting. Fill out the addresses of group members, and give one set to each graduate. If graduates are going off to college and know their new addresses, fill out cards for your group members to send to them as well. Make it as easy as you can to help group members maintain the positive relationships that have been established during the past year.

2. *Youth Group Yearbook.* Bring photos of the past year, blank books, glue, and other supplies so that kids can assemble their own "yearbooks" of the group's activities. Then have an autographing session.

How to Make Choices

BIG IDEA

To make choices wisely, you must know and trust God, and you must know and trust yourself.

BIBLE INPUT

Ruth 1:3-18
Luke 15:11-22

BRING:

Bibles
Pencils
Paper

1 *Outguess Each Other*

Remember the old rock-paper-scissors game? Each time you counted to three, you made a choice and tried to outwit the other guy. Play that same game, but on a much larger and more physical scale than just using your hands.

Pair off and have the pairs stand back to back. When the leader counts to three, the pairs spin around and face each other immediately in one of three positions:

- Gorilla—hands in the air, snarling, and growling loudly.
- Human—hands on hips and saying, "Hi there."
- Gun—draw imaginary guns from hips, shoot, and shout, "Bang."

Each pair determines who won based on the following criteria:

- Human wins over gun because a human shoots a gun.
- Gun wins over gorilla because the gorilla can be shot by a gun.
- Gorilla wins over human because the gorilla is stronger than the human.
- If both players take the same position, it's a tie.

You can play by elimination, each time with the loser sitting out until you are down to one pair. (A tie twice in a row means both lose.) Or you can just play as long as it is fun for everyone.

When you have finished playing, gather the group together and discuss the way they decided which position to play. Did they forecast what their opponent would do? Did they consider the odds?

Broaden the discussion into a discussion of general choice making.

- **What makes a choice difficult?**
- **What makes a choice simple?**

2 *Create Some Skits*

Have volunteers create several humorous skits in which the characters are asked to make choices and have difficulty doing so. One possible setting is a restaurant: the menu, the salad dressing, vegetables, fries or baked potato, what to drink, dessert. When everyone has had a chance to perform, ask:

- **In what kind of situations do you have to make choices?**
- **What are some daily choices you face?**
- **What are the big choices in your life?**
- **Do you follow any guiding principles in making a difficult choice?**
- **Are all of our choices of the same importance to God?**

3 Identify Choices

Hand out paper and pencils and have kids write the sentence below and draw a box around it.

FINISHED FILES ARE THE RESULT OF
YEARS OF SCIENTIFIC STUDY COMBINED
WITH THE EXPERIENCE OF YEARS.

Next have everyone quickly count the *F's* in the sentence. Many people don't notice all six *F's* (they overlook all the *ofs*). Sometimes the most obvious is what we overlook. Make this point as you lead into the Bible study.

Divide into study groups and have groups read one or both of the Biblical accounts below. Then have them look for the choices in these stories—the obvious choices, as well as the not so obvious. Sometimes the most obvious choices are overlooked (as in the exercise above). Don't forget God's choices. After they have listed the choices, have them list five truths about choice making.

• Ruth 1:3-18 (Naomi's choice to go home, her choice to send her daughters-in-law away, Ruth's choice to stay with Naomi, the choice of Naomi's sons to select their wives, Elimelech's choice to go to Moab, God's choice to not end the famine, to let death come, to allow the daughters to make different choices and both be all right.)

• Luke 15:11-22 (The son's choices, the father's choices, no matter how obvious they are.)

Come back together and have someone describe the basic story. Then compare lists and ask for any additions.

Finally, talk over the truths about choice making that your kids came up with. If kids don't mention it, point out that God *does* allow us to make choices. He does not manipulate or expect us to behave as automatons. We must trust Him as well as ourselves in our choice-making process.

4 Take a Break

Play this game of quick choice making to get everyone's blood going.

Arrange everyone in a circle of chairs. Select two people to stand in the middle of the circle. The goal for those two is to sit in a chair again. The goal of everyone else is to move constantly around to empty chairs to keep the two from getting a seat. If one of the two chair-seekers actually obtains a seat, the person sitting to his or her right must go to the middle of the circle and look for a seat.

Afterward, discuss how time pressure and having to consider others affects our ability to make choices.

5 *Establish Guidelines*

Distribute pencils and paper and read these choice-making guidelines. Have them jot down the ones that they consider valid. If they strongly disagree with one of the principles, ask them how they would change it to reflect truth.

- **Identify the positive and negative consequences of each choice.**
- **Paralyze yourself with the fear of failure.** (HINT: WRONG!)
- **Know what you want out of the situation.**
- **Don't make a choice anyone else will disagree with.** (HINT: Hogwash; you have to be true to yourself.)
- **Do consider how your choice will affect those closest to you.**
- **Pray for wisdom.**
- **Talk to people who may have been faced with a similar choice. Don't ask what you should do. Ask them how they worked out their choices.**
- **Trust God to lead you.**
- **If you are making a choice where a wrong choice could be fatal—don't make that choice alone. In any other case, don't be afraid to mess up.**
- **Treat every choice as if it is the most important one you'll ever make.** (HINT: Chances are you'll die early of a heart attack if you do this. In reality, not every choice is all that important. Learn to know the difference.)
- **Learn the difference between choices with short-term consequences and choices with long-term consequences. Make those choices accordingly.**

Ask your group to share some choices they are facing and close in prayer for those choices.

Optional Extras

1. *Film Clip.* Show a clip from "Indiana Jones and the Last Crusade" as a discussion starter about choices. The clip you want is the one in which Jones is in a cavern room with all the goblets and cups. At this point, another man chooses the wrong cup and horrible things happen to him. In a moment of understatement, the keeper of the room says calmly, "He chose poorly" (or something to that effect). Show as much before or after the clip as you like. Afterwards, talk about the pressure in making choices. Ask what the hardest choices are to make.

2. *Wisdom Council.* Form a council of senior citizens in your church. Invite them to come to this session and share about difficult choices they've made. Provide time for the two generations to interact with each other.

College: Christian or Secular?

BIG IDEA

Both Christian colleges and secular colleges have ministry and growth opportunities that can fit into God's plan for you. It's up to you to decide what kinds of ministry and growth opportunities you need.

BIBLE INPUT

Ecclesiastes 3:11
Matthew 5:14; 9:10-
13; 11:18, 19;
28:19, 20
John 3:17-19; 17:6-25
Romans 12:2
II Corinthians 6:17

BRING:

Bibles
Pencils
Paper
Two college
catalogs

1 Make Up College Cheers

Divide into two cheerleading squads (squads can be as small as two, or even one). Have one squad make up a cheer or a rap for an actual Christian college, and the other make up a cheer or rap for a secular college. They may choose their own schools.

When you come back together have the squads perform their cheers. After the cheers, have the groups tell how they decided to alter their cheers according to the religious status of the colleges, if they did in any way.

2 Explore the Catalogs

Use this relay to help kids get a feel for the information they can find in a college catalog. Place two college catalogs (if possible, they should be identical) at the front of the room. Number off the group so that there are two people with each number. Call out the statements below and then call out a number. Adapt the items for the catalogs you use. The two with that number should run to the front of the room to a catalog, find the item and call out the page number. Check to see if they are correct.

Find:
- the table of contents
- the first page of the index
- a reference to music course of study
- a reference to science course of study
- a faculty list
- a picture of the campus
- a history of the college
- a page about sports

3 Take a Test

Before you go to college, you often take a college entrance exam. What are some of the tests we take? (ACT, SAT, equivalency tests.)

Let's take a little test to see if we're college material.

Form a circle. The first player says a word and then counts to five (not too fast or too slow). Before he says "five," the player to the right has to say a word that begins with the last letter of the word just said, and so on. No words can be repeated.

If someone can't think of a word before the player to his or her left counts to five, he or she is given grace once. Two misses and a player is on the sidelines.

Hold a Debate

Divide into two factions. Assign each group one of these two positions.
- Everyone should go to a Christian college.
- Everyone should go to a secular college.

Have both groups look up and discuss the Scriptures below and plan a strategy for the debate. They should choose which Scriptures support their position, if any do. (Some may be used by both sides. This could be interesting.) They should also prepare a rebuttal for the Scriptures which they feel sure the other faction will use to support its position.
- Ecclesiastes 3:11—He has set eternity in human hearts.
- Matthew 5:14—you are the light of the world.
- Matthew 28:19, 20—the Great Commission.
- John 3:17-19—Jesus did not come to condemn the world.
- John 17:6-25—Jesus prays for His followers.
- Romans 12:2—the world's mold.
- II Corinthians 6:17—be separate.
- Matthew 9:10-13—why does He eat with publicans and sinners?
- Matt 11:18, 19—a friend of tax collectors and sinners.

To begin the debate let each side state its position on the issue. Alternate teams, allowing each to give one reason to support its position.

Each time you switch teams, the team can rebut the opinion just expressed by its opponents, and then state its own argument.

Take Steps toward a Decision

Have your group stand and move toward the back of the room. As you state each of these steps, have them take one step toward you. Give time for them to mentally respond to each step before going on.

First step: What is college for? An education. What kind of education do you need? Can you get it anywhere? If not, it's better to find a school with your course of study, then worry about its religious affiliation.

Second step: What kind of environment do you need personally?

Third step: Explore what kind of ministry/service activities are available at the schools you are considering. Do they reflect how you want your life to be?

Fourth step: What kind of spiritual input and support will you have?

Fifth step: Should you get your general education in one place and your specialization in another? Consider your options. If you can get a general education anywhere, should you consider a couple of years in a Christian environment?

To wrap up this session, give your kids a chance to express where they are at in terms of college. If they're . . .

- not sure yet, shrug their shoulders
- leaning toward a Christian college, lean to the right
- leaning toward a secular school, lean left
    —a community college, stand up
    —private liberal arts college, hold up two arms
    —public university, stay seated
- thinking about working for a couple of years before deciding, place hands on shoulders
- thinking about going out of state for college, stomp feet.

Close in prayer, asking God to help your group members to make wise choices and follow His plans for them.

Optional Extras

1. *College Day.* This would be a great time to plan a college day for your group. Request literature or representatives from colleges in your area and the colleges to which you would like to expose your group. Set a time for kids to look at the material and talk informally with any representatives. Also provide some information about parachurch organizations like InterVarsity, Campus Crusade, and the Navigators.

2. *Library Resources.* The public library reference section has great resources that list colleges by location, major, and any other factors you might want to consider. Take your group and have the librarian familiarize them with these resources. Allow them to take the time to research some schools or majors that strike their interest.

3. *College Life.* Invite various adults who have been to college (Christian and secular) to come to the group and talk about their experiences (academic and social) and field questions.

Violence: Should I Hit Back?

BIG IDEA

When you are attacked physically, self-protection may be the most effective and appropriate response. But when you are attacked verbally or emotionally, violence is not the answer.

BIBLE INPUT

Matthew 5:39
Luke 6:29
Psalm 86:14-17
Genesis 6:11-13
Psalm 73:6-8
Proverbs 13:2
II Corinthians 5:17-19

BRING:

Bibles
Pencils
Paper
Box of bandages
(enough for each kid
to have two)

1 Find Words in Words

Hand out pencils and paper. Call out the words below one at a time (maybe spell them too) for kids to write down. Explain: **Make as many different words as you can from each word. The words have to be at least two letters. Each person will get one point for any word that no one else has.**

Here are the words
GANG FIGHTS
AMMUNITION
VIOLENCE
PHYSICAL ABUSE
REVENGE AND RETRIBUTION
RUMBLES AND WARS.
Follow up with these questions:
- **What do each of the words we used for the game have in common?**
- **What is the definition of violence?** (Intent to hurt)
- **What are some examples of violence that you see a lot of?**
- **What kinds of violent acts are reported in the Bible?**
- **Are we ever violent to each other in ways that aren't physical?**

2 Wear Your Wounds

Give everyone an adhesive bandage and marker. Have kids write on the bandages some kind of violence that particularly disturbs them. It may have involved someone they love, or it may have happened to them. It could be verbal or physical. Have them stick the bandages on themselves in a visible place. Next, have them share about the violence in either pairs or small groups.

3 Stage a Fight

Call on several volunteers to stage a play fight like one in a movie or on TV. Let the rest of the group use a "remote" control (real or imaginary) to speed up the action, slow it down, or pause. Have one person control the remote by saying "speed," "slow," or "pause." These kids can add sound effects, too.

Have your group of volunteers perform its fight. The other members can grade each performance as to most believable, most creative, and silliest.

4 Ghostwrite for God

Have the kids read, either in small groups or individually, the Scriptures below and ghostwrite a letter from God to humankind describing how He feels about violence between people. Key ideas for each passage are in parentheses.
- Matthew 5:39; Luke 6:29 (Turn the other cheek. Don't retaliate.)
- Psalm 86:14-17 (God will defend His people. God's goodness overcomes evil.)
- Genesis 6:11-13 (God doesn't tolerate evil and will punish the wicked.)
- Psalm 73:6-8 (Evil people feel they can act violently and get away with it.)
- Proverbs 13:2 (A wise man [see verse 1] enjoys good things, but the unfaithful crave violence. Some people feed on violence.)

Debrief with questions such as these, and then have volunteers read their letters.
- **Is God a God of violence?** (This question is more complex than it looks. God does punish evildoers. Because God is perfectly just, He alone can judge the wicked. God also is compassionate and shows mercy to those who turn from evil and ask for forgiveness.)
- **Describe some ways that we are violent to (intend to hurt) each other, besides just hitting or physical violence.**
- **What alternatives do you think God has for violence?**
- **What makes it easy to respond violently?**
- **What is the difference between violence and self-defense?**

5 Do This, Do That

Play "Do This, Do That" two different ways. First, play just like "Simon Says." If the leader makes a motion and says, "Do this," the group copies. If the leader makes a motion and says, "Do that," the group ignores him or her.

Then change the rules. Have the leader say, "Do this," and make a motion (spread his arms) but this time the group should do the opposite (fold their arms). If the leader stoops down, the group should stand on their toes.

Afterward, discuss the term "an equal and opposite reaction." Point out that in the Old Testament people were told that they should react only as intensely as the situation calls for—an equal and opposite reaction. Mention the eye-for-an-eye concept in the Old Testament (Deut. 19:21). In the New Testament, we are instructed to turn the other cheek and not try to harm the other person (Matt. 5:39). That is the grace we can show someone just as God has shown us His grace.

Discuss when it's appropriate to fight back (for example, when certain rights are violated), and when it's appropriate to turn to "turn the other cheek" (for example, perhaps when you're insulted or ridiculed in some way).

Take a Self-Diagnostic Test

Have the group sit quietly as you pose the following questions. Ask them to do a self-diagnostic test to see if they are starting to depend on violence as a life-style.
- **Am I comfortable in the role of intimidator?**
- **Do I overreact in difficult situations?**
- **Do I laugh at others' pain?**
- **Do I hurt others' feelings without regret?**
- **Can I watch extreme violence and be unaffected?**
- **Can I be hurt without hurting back and walk away from the situation?**

Allow discussion to any of these questions. Point out that violence starts by a person beginning to view others as inferior to himself or herself. Thus he or she can hurt that person, either physically or emotionally, and not feel bad about it.

Apply Another Bandage

Give another adhesive bandage to each kid. Have kids write II Corinthians 5:17-19 (just the reference) on their bandages, and then read the passage aloud. After discussing ways that they can reconcile, rather than add to the violence in the world, have kids place their bandages across the other one they already stuck on themselves to form a cross, as a reminder of Christ's sacrifice to reconcile and redeem a violent world.

Close in prayer, asking God's help in making us instruments of peace.

Optional Extras

1. *Discuss Gangs.* Particularly if gangs are a problem in your area, ask some ministries to gangs come and talk about their work with kids in your community. Allow them to discuss other options for gang kids besides violence.

2. *Learn Self-defense.* Invite a self-defense instructor to come in and teach some basic self-defense moves. Have him or her discuss with your kids the difference between attack and defense, between violence and self-defense.

How Much Should I Spend on Myself?

BIG IDEA

Before you spend on yourself, you need to take care of what you owe, and what you need to invest in others, in your community, and in your future.

BIBLE INPUT

Proverbs 21:20
Luke 12:15
Mark 12:41-44
Luke 12:48
Romans 13:8

BRING:

Bibles
Pencils
Paper
Old wallet or billfold

1 Play "How's Your . . ."

When everyone is seated around the room, one player is asked to leave. While that player is out, assign to the group one of the topics below. When the player returns, she may ask only, "How's your. . .?" but she may ask as many people as she likes. Each person responds with a brief, true description (you might even require only a one-word answer) that applies to but does not name the assigned topic.

The uninformed player has a chance after every description to guess what the topic is until she has asked everyone. The last person to answer before the topic is revealed is the next to step out of the room while a new topic is assigned.

Close the game with the topics that are most closely related to spending money.
- Dog
- Hobby
- Shoes
- Parents
- Budget
- Savings account
- Income
- Money

2 Vote on Expenses

Have each kid complete this sentence on a small piece of paper: **If I were given $241, the first thing I would spend it on is. . . .**

Pass around an old wallet or billfold to collect the papers. (Depending on the size of your group you might need them to tear their papers into smaller pieces so they'll all fit into the wallet.)

Have two volunteers come to the front and empty the wallet and read the ideas one at a time. The group should give a thumbs-up or thumbs-down as to whether that idea is a good use of $241. (All opinions are valid.)

3 Describe Expenses

Have group members write down the following expense categories in random order. Discuss each category of expense. Get specific examples from your kids for each category. Prompt responses by requiring whoever you throw the wallet to to give a response. They then can throw the wallet to someone else who is required to respond. Ask questions such as:
- **What are some examples of your expenses that would fit this category?**

• **How much of your income goes to expenses in this category?**

Then ask them to prioritize the categories in this way: if they received a lump sum of money in the mail, what order would they spend it on these categories?

EXPENSE CATEGORIES

• **What you have already spent, or what you owe.**
• **What is immediately necessary for your own health and well-being.**
• **What you have promised or committed to others.**
• **What you choose to invest in the people and organizations around you.**
• **Whatever you want to spend to make your life fun.**

4 Pass the Bible

Divide into teams. Have the teams line up by height, shortest to tallest. Give the shortest person on each team a Bible. Each time you call out one of the Scripture passages listed below, the team must pass the Bible up the line. When the tallest person holds it open to the passage with his or her finger on the verse, the first part of the race is over. The first group to get the right passage to the tallest person gets one point, the second two, and so on. (Obviously, the low score when all is said and done is the winner.)

Keep in mind that the last person doesn't have to be the one to find the passage. Any one or combination of people along the line can find it. Give the teams some time to strategize.

The second part of the race is that once all the groups have found the passage and have read it among themselves, they must decide on an application from that Scripture for how much money they should spend on themselves. Do not start the race until each group has found and read the passage. Each group must write down an application and run it up to the scorekeeper. Scoring works the same as above. You might even consider requiring a 30-second time lapse before anyone can bring an answer. This will encourage some semblance of a sane answer.

Do the same thing with all four passages, then settle down to read through and discuss the applications for each Scripture. If no good applications show up, bring up those suggested ones below.

• Proverbs 21:20 (A wise person saves; a foolish person spends.)
• Luke 12:15 (Don't just acquire things.)
• Mark 12:41-44 (No matter how little you have, give.)
• Luke 12:48 (If you have a lot of resources, you're expected to be more responsible than someone without anything.)
• Romans 13:8 (Pay your debts.)

In your discussion, point out that the first principle of deciding what to spend on yourself is to realize that you can't decide that without knowing what your other responsibilities are financially—what you owe, what you need to invest in others, in your community, and in your future. Once you have taken care of these things, then you can consider spending on yourself.

5 Draw a Bill

Hand out more paper and have kids draw a dollar bill (actually any denomination of bill). They can make it look however they want, as long as it has an oval in the middle. In the oval they should draw a picture or symbol that reflects a principle of what to spend money on. This can be as farfetched or as far-reaching as they like. The important thing is to make them give some thought to the idea, not just the final product.

Take some time to share artwork and ideas, and then close in prayer.

Optional Extras

1. *Plan a Budget.* Make or get some fake money and fill the wallet or billfold with it before class. Distribute the money during class and practice making a budget. Ask your group to list their expenses as line items and estimate how much they should allow for each. List and estimate even items that their parents take care of, so that they'll see the expense.

2. *Shop the Mall.* Make a list with your kids of wants and needs. Send them to the mall for some comparison shopping. Have kids write down the prices of the items and come up with a spending plan. The group whose plan made it possible to "buy" everything on the list for the most competitive prices wins. Establish a "skimp" board of a few kids. Their task is to decide if the kids skimped in unwise places by getting a really cheap item when they should have invested a little more.

DATE USED

What Should I Wear?

BIG IDEA

Whether you like it or not, the way you dress is an expression of who you are and how you look at life. Are the messages you are sending the messages you want to be sending?

BIBLE INPUT

Exodus 28:4, 31-43
Numbers 15:37-39
I Timothy 2:9, 10
I Samuel 16:8
Matthew 26:28-30
James 2:2-4

BRING:

Bibles
Pencils
Paper
Stack of newspapers
    and tape

1 Describe Your Shoes

Have kids take off their shoes and put them in a big pile at one end of the room. Mix the shoes well. Divide into even teams and have the teams line up according to foot size.

To complete the relay the first person on each team must describe his shoes to the second person, who must then go and find the shoes, bring them back, and put them on their owner. If they are the wrong shoes, the runner goes back to the pile till he or she finds the right ones. This continues down the line until everyone has the correct shoes back and on his or her feet. First team shod wins.

2 High Fashion

You know how some outfits just *say* something. Imagine an outfit that says, "I think I am tough stuff." Or what about one that says, "I'd rather be at home in bed." The clothes we wear could be making statements about the way we see ourselves and life in general.

Keep kids in the same teams as in Step 1, and give each team a stack of newspapers, tape, and scissors. Explain the activity as follows: **Using anything in the room plus your stack of newspapers, create an outfit for someone in your group.**

Suggest some of these looks: funky, the grunge look, the Eddie Bauer-outdoorsy look, the Wall Street/Brooks Brothers look, or the private prep school look. Or kids can do their own thing and come up with their own look.

When groups have finished their fashion designs, let each group make a humorous (what else could it be?) fashion presentation, explaining its look.

3 The Biblical Look

Either in discussion groups or individually, have kids look up the following passages and write a comment or two about clothes in the Bible. Suggestions are given here in case you need them.

• Exodus 28:4, 31-43 (The priestly garments were high quality: gold, blue, purple, and scarlet yarn and fine linen; work done by professional embroiderers. These garments were sacred and gave Aaron and his sons dignity and honor.)

• Numbers 15:37-39 (Tassels actually were to remind God's people to obey His commands. In a way, the tassels were symbolic clothing.)

• I Timothy 2:9, 10 (Women were to dress modestly, not braid their hair or wear expensive jewelry and clothes. Ask group members why they think this was addressed only to women.)

• **How would you present Scripture's sense of style to the world of high fashion? Did you find any one look?** (Scripture is all across the board style-wise. From the highest quality to the symbolic to the plain and simple. The clothes people wore made statements in Bible times too.)

• **But are there any passages that tell us what to wear?**

4 Closet Organizers

Actually, God does give us some fashion tips that are sort of like classics that never go out of style. Have kids form three groups, and assign I Samuel 16:8 to one group; Matthew 6:26-30 to one; and James 2:2-4 to the third group.

Give kids a minute or two to think up creative fashion tips from these passages. Fashion tips from I Samuel 16:8 might be: Keep your heart looking good for God; People look on the outside, but God sees the real you on the inside. A fashion tip from Matthew 6:28-30 could be: Don't start obsessing about clothes; God has got you covered. A tip from James 2:2-4 might be: Don't judge people based on what they wear.

Now read the following statements to your group. Have kids indicate their level of agreement with each statement by holding up zero fingers (strongly disagree) to ten fingers (strongly agree). Discuss each statement, and have group members use the fashion tips from I Samuel 16:8; Matthew 6:28-30; and James 2:2-4 to defend their positions.

• **Christians shouldn't care about how they look or what they wear.**
• **Christians should only buy clothes that are on sale.**
• **Christians should buy clothes at places like K-Mart, not Saks Fifth Avenue.**
• **Christians shouldn't follow the latest fashion trends.**
• **Christians should dress differently than non-Christians.**

Encourage your kids to really listen to and respect each other.

5 What to Wear

Make a list with your group of the name brands that are popular in guys and girls clothes, shoes, and accessories. Also make a list of what styles of dress are popular. Have kids evaluate why those brands and styles are popular and where and when they might be appropriate or inappropriate.

Challenge kids to think about their own clothes and evaluate the messages they might be communicating. Do they need to stop buying (or start buying) certain types of clothes or accessories in light of the Scripture passages you looked at?

Say something like this: **So how do we not worry about our clothes even though we know people are checking out what we wear?** Let your kids talk about the tension between God's values and society's values.

In closing, read aloud James 2:2-4 again. Point out that as far as God's concerned, a person's clothes have nothing to do with a person's worth. We can't play favorites, just because someone is well dressed and looks good on the outside.

Optional Extras

1. *Dress-Up.* Have everyone bring funky old clothes (something they don't mind getting messed up). They should bring a woman's outfit and a man's outfit. Then when you get there (bring lots of hangers) put them all together to make a wardrobe. Let people mix and match and dress as weird or as funky as they like. Do this at the beginning and have them wear their outfits throughout the session.

2. *Advertisement Awareness.* Have each kid bring several magazines. Cut or tear out advertisements and discuss the way the person is dressed and what he or she is expressing. Also, discuss the sensual techniques used in advertising and how your group does or does not use that same type of dress.

Which Extracurricular Activities Should I Sign Up For?

BIG IDEA

Knowing what your life is all about is the first step to knowing what to add by way of extracurriculars.

BIBLE INPUT

Luke 10:38-42
Ecclesiastes 7:16-18;
8:15;10:18

BRING:

Bibles
Pencils
Paper

1 Form Animals

Note: Throughout this session, make a conscious effort to use the term "extra" as much as possible, to the point of your kids' exasperation.

Gather into a big circle or several smaller circles. Play "Elephant, Rhino, and Rabbit." This is a game that requires some "extra" help.

Choose "It." "It" stands in the middle of the circle, walks around and points to someone and says either, "Elephant," "Rhino," or "Rabbit." That person plus the two people beside him or her must respond in one of three ways, depending on what animal has been called.

• Elephant: Middle person puts both fists end to end to his nose to make a trunk. Each side person puts an open hand to the middle person's ear to make a floppy elephant's ear.

• Rhino: Middle person puts fists together at her nose with index fingers pointing to make a rhino horn. Each side person puts a fist to the middle person's ear to make a rhino's stubby ears.

• Rabbit: Middle person puts hand behind back to make a bunny tail. Each side person puts a fist with index finger pointing up to the middle person's ear to make rabbit ears.

As soon as "It" has called out the name of the animal, he or she counts to ten as fast as possible. This game makes for some good laughs. When someone messes up, he or she becomes the next "It."

Point out the "extra" help it requires to make each animal, and how much more challenging and more fun it makes the game.

2 Draw a Pizza

Give everyone pencils and paper. Have them draw as large a circle as possible on both sides of the paper. Say something like: **By its very makeup the word "extra-curricular" implies that you are adding on to something else. You start with a base; then you decide what to add. Let's say you have a pizza crust and sauce. What can you add to make different kinds of pizza?** Have the kids draw their favorite kind of pizza in one of the circles on the paper.

What are some other bases to which you can add different extras? (Cookies, ice cream sundaes, salads, clothes, computer software/hardware, etc.)

What would happen if you added chocolate chips to pizza sauce or pepperoni to cookie dough? (Yuk!) **The first step to knowing what your extras should be is knowing what your base is.**

Turn over the pages and fill in the circles with all kinds of extracurriculars as kids are familiar with. Have them fill in their own circle first, then compare together all the activities or clubs others have listed.

3 Decide on Your Base

What makes up the base of a pizza? (Flour, eggs, water, oil, etc.) Some people put sesame seeds on their pizza. The sesame seeds are extra. You can take away the sesame seeds and you still have pizza crust. But if you take away the flour, do you still have pizza crust? No. Flour is so significant to pizza crust that there would be no crust without it.

What are the parts of your life that are so significant that your life would not be the same life without them? This tells you what your base is. Give the kids some time to think about this. Give them another piece of paper and have them draw a big circle. At the bottom of the page have them write down the parts of their life they consider vital. This time have them divide the circle into pizza pieces proportionate to each of their significant items (family, girlfriend or boyfriend, music or sports, important hobbies, church). Encourage them to think it through before they start sizing the pieces.

After they have finished drawing, have each person explain to another person or to a small group what the pizza crust or base of his or her life is.

4 Evaluate the Pizza

The first question to ask about your pizza is this: Are there too many pieces? Am I spread too thin? Are there too few? Do I need more interests?

Have the kids turn over their papers and write the following words down either margin with a dotted line between each pair. Have them leave plenty of room between each pair

people. . . . . solitude
physically active . . . . very still
no-brainer . . . . mentally active
fun . . . . serious

Have the kids jot down where each piece of their pizzas would fall on each continuum, noting if any one area is out of balance. For instance, if all the pieces fall on the still end of the active/still continuum, that should be noted. Say something like this: **Once you know what your life is made of, then you must decide what you need to add to it. If everything about your life is people-oriented, then you must decide if that means you need something quiet to balance your life (the Chess club or symphony) or does it mean that you are outgoing and should choose something lively and interactive (the pep squad or jazz band)? First you must know what your life is made of—the pizza crust—then decide what you need to add to it.**

Give your kids some time to make notes and to think about what they might need. Small discussion groups might be a good tool for evaluation.

5 Add Your Extras

Have kids read the following Scripture passages. For each passage, kids should come up with a question, based on the passage, that could be used in evaluating whether or not to take on an extracurricular activity. For example:

- Luke 10:38-42—Are you too busy?
- Ecclesiastes 8:15—Will you enjoy it?
- Ecclesiastes 7:16-18—Is your life in balance?
- Ecclesiastes 10:18—Are you doing enough?

As you close, ask these questions to help kids evaluate their current activities.

- **Can you overdose on being involved at church?**
- **What difference does it make if God is your base? Are there some activities that you might choose over others?**

Give kids a minute or two to think about their answers, and then pray, asking God to help all of you to focus on Him in everything you do.

Optional Extras

1. *Make Pizza.* Make pizza with English muffins, pizza sauce, and a buffet of toppings. Label each topping as an extracurricular activity your kids will be seeing in school this year.

2. *Present Extracurriculars.* Give kids who are already a part of extracurriculars one minute each to talk about the sport or club they are a part of. Have them tell what they have enjoyed about it and how they chose it.

Choosing the Best Friends

BIG IDEA

Friends are not only the people we like most, but also the people we become most like.

BIBLE INPUT

Proverbs 27:17; 22:24, 25; 17:17; 27:6; 27:14; 19:6

BRING: Bibles
Pencils
Paper

1 Match Behavior

Note: Before this meeting, pull aside two friends and clue them in on the mind reading game in Step 2 so that they can be the leader and the mind reader.

As the kids arrive, whisper to each of them one of the actions listed below and ask them not to tell anyone else the action they've been assigned. Try to distribute the actions evenly.

- Pinch
- Slap
- Tickle
- Step on toes
- Scratch behind ears
- Rub head

Start the game by saying something like: **Often when we look for friends, we look for someone who is like us in some way. We want to have something in common. Find the other people in the room who were given the same action as you, but without talking. Do your action only.**

After the groups are formed, have them stay seated in groups while you discuss the following questions:

- **Was it hard to find the other people in your group?**
- **Did you find some by watching rather than walking up to them?**
- **Did this game reflect in any way what it is like to make friends?** (You find people who act like you and join them.)
- **Are there any drawbacks to this way of making friends?** (You might never become different because you're always with people who are like you.)

2 Watch a Mind Reader

Not only do we look for friendships with people who are already like us, we become like our friends the longer we know them. We think like them, talk like them—sometimes we even seem to read each other's minds. Let's test that with some friends.

Call the two friends you clued in before class to the front. Have the mind reader leave the room and have the group pick an object in the room for the leader to think about and test the mind reader with.

When the mind reader returns to the room, the leader points to many objects in a row. The mind reader stops him when he points to the object the group chose.

How did he know? The leader should always point to a black (or any color you decide upon) object before pointing to the chosen object.

Have them play several times and even switch roles. If anyone else asks to try the mind reader part, let him. Play until someone guesses or lets the cat out of the bag.

3 Discuss Scriptures

Have the discussion groups you formed in the opening activity tackle the Scriptures below, answering for each one: What are one or two things about friendship we can pick up from this Scripture?
- Proverbs 27:17 (Iron sharpens iron; friends make each other better.)
- Proverbs 22:24, 25 (Don't be friends with an angry man; you pick up friends' habits; be careful of the bad ones.)
- Proverbs 17:17 (A friend loves at all times; a friend is not for you one day, then against you the next.)
- Proverbs 27:6 (Friends tell us the truth even if it doesn't feel good; friends want us to become better people.)
- Proverbs 27:14 (Don't push your friend; don't be rude or "loud in the morning.")
- Proverbs 19:6 (This is a tricky one: Does "friend" really mean "friend"? Some people act like your friend to get something from you.)

4 Invent Oxymorons

An oxymoron (ox-ee-MOH-ron) is a combination of words with opposite meanings, such as jumbo shrimp, pretty ugly, etc. See how many oxymorons your group can think of. Afterwards say something like: **Is this an oxymoron: bad friend?**
- **Is there such a thing as a bad friend?**
- **What would be characteristic of a bad friend?**
- **Why would we choose to have a bad friend?**
- **What keeps us in a relationship once we determine it is bad for us?**
- **How can bad friendships hurt us?**
- **How do we get out of relationships that are harmful to us?**

5 Evaluate Friendship Patterns

Have kids do a self-diagnostic test, either on paper or mentally, as you call out these questions:
- **How many of my friendships would I call "bad" friendships?**
- **What kind of people am I drawn to in developing friendships?**
- **Do most of my friends put as much energy into the friendship as I do?**
- **Do any of my friends put more energy into the friendship than I do?**
- **Are there any hurtful friendships that I am staying in for some reason?**

 • If so, what are the reasons?
 • Who could I build healthy relationships with to replace the unhealthy ones I have?

Write a Letter

Have everyone write a short letter to someone who has been a good friend. Ask the kids to identify in the letter the specific ways that person has been a good friend and to express thanks for the friendship.

Close in prayer, praying for each other to be good friends and to find good friends.

Optional Extras

1. *Invite "Old Friends."* Look for a pair of long-time female friends and long-time male friends among the senior citizens in your church. Have them come and talk about finding good friends and being a good friend. Allow questions if your guests say it is OK.

2. *Read a Book.* Read the Shel Silverstein book *The Giving Tree* or any other book that is appropriate to the topic. Start a discussion of why friends are important to your kids.

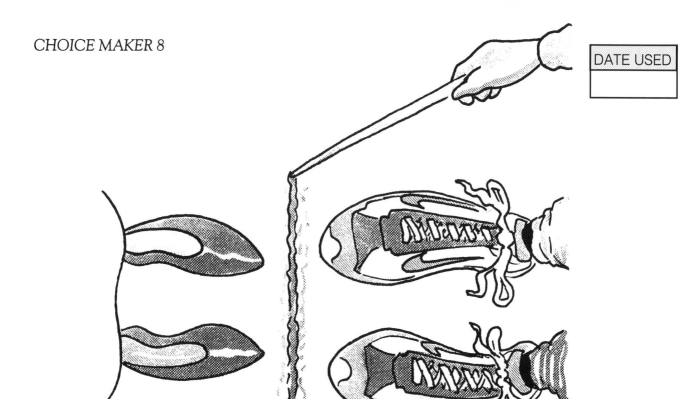

DATE USED

Sex: Where Should I Draw the Line?

BIG IDEA

When our physical affection for each other moves from being an expression of our own affection to an intent to arouse the other person or ourselves, we have crossed the line to sexual foreplay.

BIBLE INPUT

I Corinthians 6:12-20
Ephesians 5:3
I Thessalonians 4:3-5

BRING:

Bibles
Pencils
Paper
Duct tape

1 *Get a Smile*

Note: You might want to conduct this session with separate groups of guys and girls. If you do, skip Step 1. The language is quite forthright, so adjust it to fit your group.

Play "Honey, if you love me, smile." Sit in a large circle with "It" in the middle of the circle. He may approach anyone without touching that person and say three times, "Honey, if you love me, smile." If the person smiles, she becomes the new "It." If she keeps from smiling, "It" must keep trying. If your group is large, play in more than one circle at a time.

2 Walk the Line

Make a zigzag line on the floor with duct tape. Recruit a volunteer to close his or her eyes and walk the line, listening to the cues from the rest of the group.

When the walker steps to the right of the line the group beeps at him. When he steps to the left of the line the group boings at him. The group must beep and boing the line-walker from one end of the line to the other. Change line-walkers when the first person gets good at walking the line.

• **What made it hard to stay on the line?** (If it doesn't come up in conversation, mention the fact that the line was so thin.)

• **Have you heard the expression "There's a fine line between (this) and (that)?" What are some things in life that there is a fine line between?** (Gossip and sharing a concern; cheating on homework and helping a lot.)

• **How does the "fine line" relate to the physical part of a dating relationship?**

• **What is on each side of the fine line?**

• **What makes stepping over the fine line wrong?**

• **What makes not stepping over the fine line hard to do?**

3 Write Press Releases

Divide into groups, and have each group read I Corinthians 6:12-20, Ephesians 5:3, and I Thessalonians 4:3-5. When groups have finished, discuss these questions.

• **Why do you think God's Word goes to such extremes about sexual immorality?** Let kids express their opinions. Point out that God created us as sexual beings and He knows the power of sexual attraction. He also knows that people can abuse sex and never think about their sexual partners. Instead of getting caught in unhealthy relationships, God says to get out of the situation fast.

•**Is God anti-sex? Why or why not?** Paul described the body as the temple of the Holy Spirit. Our bodies (or someone else's) have dignity as created beings and as new creations in Christ. God's goal for us is purity and holiness. He elevates sexual intercourse to an expression of love between a husband and wife.

Next, each group should write a press release announcing God's view of sexual immorality, and then read it to the whole group. Make this almost skit-like. Groups can created sound effects like typewriters, or interrupt a regularly scheduled program with an emergency broadcast to give the press release.

4 Define Sexual Immorality

Take the duct tape again and make a straight line down the middle of the floor. Label one side "sexual immorality" and the other side "sexual morality." Write the phrases below on separate sheets of paper and ask the kids to place the sheets on the appropriate side of the line, or on the line if they feel it's not immoral, but could become so. Allow discussion on each choice. Review these and eliminate those you wouldn't be comfortable talking about with your group. Add others if you feel it's appropriate. You know your kids better than we do. Our intent is not to titillate, but to provide honest discussion.

- a kiss on the cheek
- a kiss on the lips
- running your hands over your date's body
- a long, deep, passionate kiss
- holding hands
- putting your arms around each other
- sitting close together
- hugging
- touching your girlfriend's breasts (or allowing your boyfriend to touch your breasts)
- kissing your girlfriend's breasts (or allowing your boyfriend to kiss your breasts)
- lying beside each other in the dark watching TV
- making out for over an hour in a private place
- making out for ten minutes in the front seat of a car
- sleeping together overnight with no intent to have sex
- taking off some of your clothes when you make out
- taking off all of your clothes when you make out

5 Drawing the Line

Point out that sex is not just the actual time when a boy is inside of a girl. It is a process where they both work up sexual intensity with the culmination being intercourse. Just because they don't get that far doesn't mean they haven't started the process that we call sex or making love. Sex outside of marriage is wrong according to Scripture, no matter what your age or level of commitment.

Divide into guys and girls and read the case studies below. Have each gender discuss the case studies, and then send a representative up to stand on the moral side, the immoral side, or on the line of tape for about to cross over.

CASE ONE: Jen and Tom have dated since junior high. They've dated so long they feel married. When Jen house-sat last summer Tom practically moved in just like her husband. Sex is pretty old hat to them. It was fun at first sneaking around, but now they're used to it and it's not as exciting as it used to be.

CASE TWO: Karen and Cindy both have had boyfriends and enjoyed making out. But lately they've been curious about what it would be like to be with another girl. There must be some reason people do it that way. They've started sort of talking around it, but they haven't done anything about it yet.

CASE THREE: Sarah is proud of the fact that she's a virgin. She gets into heavy physical stuff. Her reputation is that she'll do anything a guy asks her to—to him. So far she has found a way to stop things before he's actually inside her. Usually she can distract him with her willingness to make him feel good.

CASE FOUR: David and Teresa have decided to wait until they are married to have sex. Sometimes David wants to have sex with Teresa so bad he won't be alone with her in his house because it would be too convenient. They still have two years until they can even think about getting married, but they are planning on waiting, even though waiting is difficult.

With representatives still on the lines, close in prayer asking God to help your kids flee from sexual immorality.

Optional Extras

1. *AIDS Awareness.* This may be an ideal time to have someone to talk with your kids about AIDS and other sexually transmitted diseases.

2. *Soap Talk.* Videotape a soap opera or two. Play it back in fast-forward and have kids keep a running tally of sexual images they see (either in the program itself or the commercials.) Talk about how we are bombarded with sexual images. Point out that 97% of the sexual encounters in soap operas are between people who aren't married to each other.

When Is It OK to Tell a Secret?

BIG IDEA You should betray a confidence only when keeping the secret will cause more harm than breaking it.

BIBLE INPUT Proverbs 25:9, 10; 11:13; 20:19; 17:9; 13:3; 18:19

BRING: Bibles
Pencils
Paper

1 Shoot Secret Victims

Explain: **There is a secret to how this game works. See if you can figure it out.** The leader points to someone and says, "Bang, you're dead." The group then must guess who was shot.

The most obvious choice is the person the leader pointed to. The secret, though, is that the person who was shot is the person who speaks first after the "gunfire." Of course you don't want to announce who has been shot immediately after the first person talks. Let the guessing go on for a while, then announce who was shot. By then hardly anyone will remember who spoke first.

Play several rounds until someone guesses the secret, then debrief with questions such as the following.
- What was the secret in this game?
- What are the characteristics of a secret?
- What are you saying about a person if you say he or she can keep a secret?
- What are you saying about a person if you say he or she can't keep a secret?
- Does it cost something to keep a secret? What?
- Who does the secret belong to? Who has the right to reveal it or not reveal?
- Why do people choose to share their own secrets with someone else?
- Why do people choose to share someone else's secret?

2 Discuss Case Studies

Read or have someone read these case studies out loud to the group. Ask for their assessment of the decision to reveal or not reveal the secret involved. What factors would they have to consider in the decision?

Case One: Amy was the new girl at school. She really wanted everyone to like her, but her clothes weren't as nice as the other girls' and she just didn't seem as "together." When the girls saw Amy coming they often joked about her appearance until she was within earshot.

One day the girls decided it would be really funny to invite Amy to a dressy party, but tell her it was casual. They wondered if she would even notice that she was dressed differently than everyone else.

One of the girls, Beth, is having doubts about this joke they are playing on Amy. This secret just seems too hurtful. Beth is wondering if she should betray her friends just to save some embarrassment for this girl that she doesn't even really like.

Case Two: David has been in and out of drug rehab centers since he was thirteen years old. He would stay clean for a while, but inevitably would get with some friends (at least that's what he called them) who provided him with the liquor or the drugs to break down his resistance.

This time David's been clean for about a month and a half. But the other day his brother Jonathan found a fifth of whiskey in David's drawer. When Jonathan confronted David, David said it was just in case he got the jitters. David asked Jonathan to please keep this secret for him.

Case Three: Mollie and Trish had been classmates for five or six years. They also went to the same church. They had never spent a lot of time together, but because they had known each other so long Trish felt free to ask Mollie privately why she was coming to school with so many bumps and bruises.

Mollie immediately began to cry. She needed someone to talk to. She said her dad had been drinking and had hurt her several times recently. Sometimes she was scared to be home with him alone. She didn't know what he would do.

Trish was shocked, but not as shocked as when she went to church Sunday and saw Mollie's dad's name in the church bulletin. He was supposed to be appointed to be an elder in the church in the coming month. Trish now had an awful secret.

Case Four: Daniel was stopped by the police last Friday night for a traffic violation. Daniel didn't want anyone to know, but he confided it in Felicia, his study partner. Felicia felt so honored that Daniel trusted her. Maybe he did like her after all. She wanted to tell her friends so they could reassure her that Daniel liked her. Should she tell his secret?

3 Paraphrase Scripture

Break into teams to look up the Scripture passages below, and then paraphrase each as a teenager in Bible days would have written it.
- Proverbs 25:9, 10 (Don't betray a confidence.)
- Proverbs 11:13 (A gossip betrays a confidence.)
- Proverbs 20:19 (Avoid someone who talks too much.)
- Proverbs 17:9 (Repeating a secret separates friends.)
- Proverbs 13:3 (Guard your lips.)

After all the Scriptures have been paraphrased, compare group responses.

As a large group, make up a list of principles of when to tell a secret based on these Scriptures.

4 Keep or Tell?

Read Proverbs 18:19. **If you reveal a secret, someone is probably going to be offended. Before you decide to tell a secret, make sure that the person you are going to hurt by revealing it will only be hurt worse if you keep it.**

Have kids think of examples of secrets that would be worth revealing. Then have them think of secrets that aren't worth revealing.

Provide a time at the end of class for group members who might have betrayed the confidence of someone else to go and ask forgiveness.

Optional Extras

1. Gossip. Play that old game, "Gossip." Start a statement around a circle, having each person whisper it to the next person. They only get one chance to whisper it. See what the statement has become by the time it has gone all the way around the circle. Point out that with many secrets shared, this is what happens. The secret becomes something different the more it is shared.

2. Secret Passing. Divide into two teams. Give each team a sheet of paper. This sheet of paper is their "secret." They may fold the paper in any way they want. Both teams mingle among each other, passing the paper as many times as possible to another team member without being seen. When one team finally catches the other team passing their secret, separate the teams back out. Count how many people passed the secret during the game. Give one point to the team who blew the whistle on their opponent. Then give each team as many points as people who had passed the paper on that team.

Christian Rock vs. Secular Rock

 **BIG IDEA**
"Christian" and "secular" are probably not the best labels by which to evaluate your music. "Immoral" and "moral" may be better.

 **BIBLE INPUT**
Ephesians 5:3-20

 **BRING:**
Bibles
Pencils
Paper
Boom box with tape
    player

1 Pass Open or Closed

Seat the group in a large circle and pass around the boom box, letting people open or close the door to the cassette part of it. As each person passes it he says either, "I pass it open," or, "I pass it closed."

The leader must then tell whoever is doing the passing if he is correct. Whether the cassette door is open or closed is not the point. The criteria for passing open or closed is whether the person passing it has his legs crossed or uncrossed. Crossed = closed. Uncrossed = open.

You can play this in one of two ways. You can play until the group guesses what criterion the leader is using—then the game is over. Or you can send several people out of the room, explain the game to the group, and have the people come in one at a time, observe the game, and try to guess the criterion. This makes the game last a little longer.

After the game, debrief with questions such as:

• **To those of us who weren't in the know, what was the obvious meanings of the labels "open" and "closed"?**

• **What did the labels "open" and "closed" actually mean?**

• **What did we have to do in order to figure out the meaning of those labels?** (Watch closely, find a pattern, associate the patterns, and play long enough to put it all together.)

2 Define Your Terms

Discuss:

• **What kind of labels do we use when we talk about music or songs?** (Rock, country, top ten, classical, blues, Christian, secular, gospel, soul.)

• **Sometimes we call a song "good" or "bad". What can the label "good song" mean?** (Music I like, classically correct, better than I could do, I agree with it, I like the words, I like the music, I like the beat.)

• **What can the label "bad song" mean?** (I don't like it, stupid words, crummy music, immoral words, negative ideas.)

• **What does the label "rock music" mean to you?**

• **What do the labels "Christian music" and "secular music" mean?** (Explore all ideas: the lyrics, the music, the artist, the songwriter.) Invite disagreement and discussion.

• **What, if anything, makes music Christian or secular?**

• **What, if anything, makes lyrics Christian or secular?**

• **Can a person who does not believe in God write a "Christian" song?**

3 Discover Biblical Guidelines

Give pairs or small groups the following directions to study Ephesians 5:3-20.

• **Make a list of all the words that describe qualities God does *not* desire to see in His children.**

• **List two songs that you would have to exclude from your listening library if you wanted to have only music that exemplifies the qualities you just listed.**

• **Why do you think someone is an idolator if he is immoral, impure, or greedy? (vs. 5)**

• **What is an example of the "empty words" spoken of in verse 6? How can we be deceived by "empty words?"**

• **Make a list of modern day examples of deeds of darkness.**

• **Make a list of deeds of light.**

• **Can goodness, righteousness, and truth be fun to sing about or good to listen to?**

• **Name some songs that are about, or include, goodness, righteousness, and truth.** (Look for Christian and secular music.)

• **Are there songs today that fit the description in verse 12?**

• **Write a modern paraphrase of verse 19.**

• **In verse 20, what are we supposed to thank God for? Can that include everyday kind of stuff?**

• **Are there "secular" songs that celebrate God's gifts even though they aren't hymns?**

• **According to this Scripture, what are the criteria for the kinds of music you should listen to and what are the criteria for the kind of music you should avoid?**

4 Play Musical Chairs

Play the old game musical chairs. Arrange a circle of chairs with one less chair than there are people. As players walk inside the circle of chairs, play music on the boom box; then suddenly stop the music. Everyone sits when the music stops. The one person without a chair is out. Remove that person and one chair from the circle and start the music again. Play until there are two people and one chair.

As a twist, play bits from several songs. If kids think a song is moral, they should move clockwise. If they think it's immoral, they should move counterclockwise. It's okay if they disagree and move in different directions.

When you have a winner, come back together again as a group and close the session with discussion.

5 Compare Labels

In our opening game we had to identify labels for how we were passing a boom box. Actually the labels we were using had nothing to do with the boom box. They described something else altogether.

Sometimes we use the terms "Christian music" and "secular music" like we did the terms "open" and "closed" in the game.

Don't just assume that Christian music is good and secular music is bad. Evaluate all the music you listen to.

- Are the words moral?
- Does the song put down other people?
- Does the song celebrate life?

Ask the group for suggestions of the kinds of songs God loves for us to listen to.

Optional Extras

1. *Banana Lip Sync.* Allow the kids to bring some of their favorite songs to lip sync. Provide bunches of bananas for microphones and let the concert begin.

2. *Life and Music.* Have the kids do research on their favorite artists, Christian or not. Have them bring a report (written or verbal) to class telling about how that artist's life-style fits in with what he or she sings.

DATE USED

School: Drop Out, Skip Out, or Stay In?

BIG IDEA

Whether it is skipping school or dropping out, consider two things carefully: your reasons why, and your options if you do. Ask yourself, "Will this increase or decrease my options in life?"

BIBLE INPUT

Luke 15:11-20

BRING:

Bibles
Pencils
Paper

1 Count to Twenty

Some of the first things you learned in school were your ABCs and how to count. Let's see how well you do. Divide the group in half. Designate one side the "S's and T's." Designate the other side as the "every other letters" side. Have the whole group count to twenty out loud. When the number starts with an S or a T, that team should stand. If the number doesn't start with an S or a T, the other group should stand. Go slowly at first. Once they get that down, sit in a circle and go around the circle, counting to twenty again and again as quickly as possible. This time, individual team members stand or stay seated, depending on the number. Eliminate those who mess up.

2 Play Password

Use the words listed below to stage some games of Password. For each game, choose two teams of two. Whisper or write the same word to one person on each team. These players take turns giving one-word clues to try to get their partners to guess what the word is. If the players give more than four clues each, start a new word. Whoever guesses three out of five first wins that round. If your group is small enough, have an elimination tournament.

Report	Grades	School
Teacher	Study	Hooky
Skip	Homework	Pass
Cafeteria	Homeroom	Principal
Textbooks	Friends	Class
Lunch	Locker	Cheerleader
Homecoming	Sports	Ball game
School bus	Playground	Gym

After the game, ask what all the words had in common. If you want to play longer, ask the group for words relating to school and use their written suggestions.

3 Design Skits

Assign small groups the skits below. Each skit involves a present and in-the-future scene. The future scene should involve the main characters talking about their habits in high school and whether they are still affected by those habits. Give the groups five to ten minutes to prepare their skits and then come together to present them to the rest of the group.

• PRESENT—Don hates school. In fact, by the time eighth grade rolled around he was cutting as much as he was there. By tenth grade he's working at Dairy Queen full time. Show us Don's life ten years later.

• PRESENT—Claire is a B+ student. She works hard, but has fun too. She finishes school with a 3.25 G.P.A. and has plans to go to college. Show us Claire's life ten years later.

• PRESENT—Rachel is blowing off school. She buys homework, cheats on tests, and plays hooky as often as possible. She'll graduate, just barely, and will be *really* ready to party then. How will she be partying in ten years?

Study Scripture

Part of your decision to participate in school has to do with whether you are willing to work through appropriate channels. There is no school without problems. You will be required to study things that you may never use again. But an education is important enough that there are laws requiring you to have one. Whether you can work through the appropriate channels and graduate from school is an indicator of whether you can work through channels in the rest of society and the rest of life.

Prepare the group to discuss the parable of the lost son by saying something like: Before there were public schools, there were agricultural communities. Instead of the kids' leaving home each day to go to school, they stayed at home each day to keep the farm and learn the trade. Then they either took over the family business or went on to start their own similar businesses. Jesus told a parable of a son who didn't want to work through these channels. By trying to skip out on the things he needed to learn while growing up, he decreased his options.

Read together Luke 15:11-20.

• What learning opportunities did the younger son skip out on?
• Was he ready to leave and make wise choices with his resources?
• Do you think the father did the right thing in letting him go?
• What do you think the father could have done differently?
• What made the son decide to go home?
• Do you think the father had any inheritance left to give him?
• How could the son have chosen differently?
• What do you think made him want to skip out?
• Did leaving "school" increase or decrease the younger son's options?

Discuss Dropping Out

• **What makes a person want to drop out of school?** Point out that it's easy to believe there's more out there for you to do.
• **Does dropping out of school increase or decrease your options in life?**

• **Does skipping school increase or decrease your options in life?**
• **What, if any, are the positive outcomes of dropping out of school?**

Close this session by saying something like: **Life is hard enough on any of us without us decreasing our own options. Graduating from school gives you the greatest potential. Before you start skipping or dropping out, talk with someone. Don't just run away from responsibility and mess up your chances.**

Optional Extras

1. *Guest Speaker.* Invite a teen counselor who works with dropouts to come and talk about the options, or lack of them, kids have when they leave school early.

2. *Support System.* Teach the kids to look out after each other in school, by checking on each other and praying for each other. Maybe even establish a buddy system for those who are struggling the most. Consider peer counseling and tutoring at the church after school.

To Drink or Not?

BIG IDEA The first question is, should you get drunk? The second question is, if you shouldn't get drunk, then should you drink?

BIBLE INPUT

Galatians 5:19-21
Luke 21:34
Romans 13:13, 14

BRING:

Bibles
Pencils
Paper
A wine glass

1 Run Relays

Before breathalizer tests, a person stopped for driving under the influence of alcohol was asked to do a couple of coordination tests. He or she may have been asked to walk a straight line heel-to-toe or to hold his or her arms straight out and then touch the nose.

We're going to do some relays that will require some coordination.

1. Place a chair in the middle of the group. Have each team line up side by side, forming a box around the chair. The object is for the first member of each team to run from his or her place, around the chair, and to the other end of his or her team. Each team member should do likewise until the team is in its original position. The obvious kicker is that the runners will often get to the chair in the middle at the same time. It takes coordination not to just run over each other.

2. Give everyone two pieces of paper to tear in half. Assign some fixed point for the runners to reach and return from. To get to the point, the participant must only step on his or her pieces of paper. That means stepping on the first piece, laying the second one down in front of him, stepping on that piece, picking up the first piece (while standing on one foot), and moving it ahead, and so on.

- How would these games have been different if all of us had been drunk?
- How does being drunk affect people physically? Emotionally? Mentally?
- When people are stopped for drunk driving it's called DUI, that is, driving under the influence. When a person is drunk, in what ways is he influenced?

2 Reason Why

Say something like: Obviously, there are reasons why people want to drink alcohol rather than Sprite or Coke. If not, there wouldn't be as many people drinking as there are. And as unpleasant as a hangover feels and looks, there is something about getting drunk that makes it worth it to a lot of people. Let's get honest about some of those reasons.

Distribute pencils and paper and have each person complete one of the following sentences on small pieces of paper.

- One reason people drink alcohol instead of a nonalcoholic beverage is. . . .
- One reason people get drunk is. . . .

Have the kids fold up their sentences and put them in the wine glass as it is passed.

When all the sentences are collected, have volunteers read them aloud to the group. The group may respond with a happy "ding-ding-ding" (like on a game show) if the answer is true (even if it isn't an acceptable answer to someone personally). If the answer is not true they may respond with a deep "buzz." If there is a difference of opinions, ask for reasons.

If it doesn't come up in the reasons, point out that one of the reasons people get drunk is to run away from the hard realities of life. While there is nothing wrong with comforting yourself, to comfort yourself with something that will make you less able to deal with reality is not a smart move.

 # Check the Bible

Drinking and getting drunk, while definitely related, are two different things. In the Biblical culture, wine was a common beverage, partly because of the dirty, unhealthy water. But the Bible does have some things to say about drunkenness and getting drunk.

Have students read the Scriptures below and state God's opinion of drinking so much that you impair your senses or, in other words, get drunk.
- Galatians 5:19-21
- Luke 21:34
- Romans 13:13, 14

Have someone describe the feeling of being drunk. (We're not sure any of your kids will want to sit there and admit that they know how being drunk feels. You might want to invite an older person who doesn't drink any longer to this session.)

Then have someone describe a hangover and what makes it worth drinking again after being so sick.

Debate the Point

Divide the group in half and ask them to respond to this question: **If getting drunk is foolish and unnecessary, should people drink at all?** Assign the group on your right the "yes" position. Assign the group on your left the "no" position.

Give them five minutes to decide their arguments, and then let them come out fighting. Each side must state its reasons and let the other side rebut those reasons.

When both sides are out of reasons, have the kids come together and state their personal feelings. Provide a safe environment in which they can share their experiences with alcohol and their curiosity, fascination, or disgust with it.

If you have children of alcoholics in your group, give them time to share how alcohol abuse affects the people around the person who drinks.

As you conclude the discussion, remind young people that God calls Christians to obey the law. Whether or not they feel drinking (without getting drunk) is OK for mature adults, young people need to acknowledge that underage drinking is illegal and contrary to God's will.

TO DRINK OR NOT?

Optional Extras

1. *Call the Police!* Invite a police officer to come and tell your kids about the penalty for driving under the influence. Have him also tell of any of his experiences with drunk drivers.

2. *Make Posters.* Provide art materials and have the kids make posters to support helping their friends not to drive drunk. Vote on the most creative, the most effective, and the most artistic.

Choosing Whether to Become a Christian

BIG IDEA

Becoming a Christian means trusting Jesus enough to invite Him permanently into your life.

BIBLE INPUT

Romans 8:29-39
John 14:23-26
I John 3:1

BRING:

Bibles
Pencils
Paper
Piece of fabric or bag of blindfolds

1 Run Streets and Alleys

Streets and Alleys is a tag game. "It" chases another player though a maze of people that is constantly changing from streets to alleys.

To form the maze, position all but two players who are running the maze in a row, holding hands with the people beside them. This formation makes the alleys through which "It" chases the other player.

There is one more catch. The leader stands outside the maze and shouts one of two instructions. When the leader shouts, "Streets!" the people making up the maze turn a quarter turn to their right and grasp hands again in the other direction. When the leader shouts, "Alleys!" the maze returns to its original formation.

All this while, "It" may not cross the joined hands, but the one being chased may duck under or do whatever to keep from being tagged.

Afterward, gather the group together and say something like: **Tonight we are going to talk about the choice to become a Christian. Sometimes the path to a personal relationship to God can seem like a maze. We hear so many different rules, then just when we're almost there, it seems like someone changes the rules. One minute we hear that God loves us unconditionally. Then we hear that we must obey for God to bless us. It can be very confusing. We need to take a simple look tonight at what being a Christian is from God's viewpoint.**

2 Write a Letter

Have everyone write a short letter from God to humanity telling what kind of relationship He would like to have with them.

Share the letters in pairs or small groups.

3 Trust Your Partner

A key word in our relationship with God is *trust*. If you don't trust someone, it's hard to think he'll take care of you. Let's play a game to see what it feels like to trust.

Play trust tag. The object of the game is like regular tag except that everyone is in partners, with one partner blindfolded. Tear the fabric into blindfolds or hand out ready-made blindfolds. The blindfolded partner holds on to the waist of the seeing partner. The seeing partner shouts directions to the blindfolded partner. The object is for the blindfolded player to tag another blindfolded player.

After you play, discuss what it was like to trust the other player. Discuss from both perspectives, seeing and blindfolded.

4 Discuss Scripture

Becoming a Christian has a lot to do with trust. In any relationship you need to be able to trust some things about the other person.
- What does it mean to trust a friend?
- When you say someone is trustworthy, what are some other words to describe it?

When you build a relationship with God, you have to figure out who He says He is, then if He *is* who He says He is, and finally, if He will consistently stay that way.

Have small groups read together Romans 8:28-39, then discuss the following points:
- What things does this passage say about God that display to you His trustworthiness?
- What is God's purpose for us, according to verse 29?
- What evidence does verse 32 give to show God's love for us?
- How is Jesus pulling for us, according to verse 34?
- List the things that cannot separate us from Christ's love.
- Discuss what things, if any, you or other people might think *can* separate us from Christ's love.

If the discussion times have taken a bit of concentration, you might consider having a sort of Chinese fire drill and mixing up groups before reading the next passage.

Have the small groups read through John 14:23-26.
- Under what conditions does God make His home in someone?
- What does it mean to love God?
- What does it mean to obey God?
- What would it mean for you if God made His home inside you?
- What would it mean for you to think that the Holy Spirit, sent from God, was active in you all the time?

5 Interview Christians

Ask for volunteers to be interviewed (rather than just giving testimonies) about what it was like to become a Christian. Start with the following questions, then let the group ask questions.
- When did you first think you wanted to be a Christian?
- How did you go about inviting God to make His home in you?
- What does being a Christian mean to you in everyday life?

6 Pray

Read I John 3:1.

Say something like: **One of the greatest acts of faith is to pray to God. Just praying expresses faith in a God that we cannot see and sometimes cannot feel. We can pray to God either mentally or verbally and express our faith in Him, and invite Him to make His home in us.**

Lead the group in prayer. Take this opportunity to see if any group members are ready to invite Jesus into their lives.

Optional Extras

1. *Hear from the Pastor.* Invite your pastor to come and talk to your kids about what being a Christian means to him.

2. *Walk the Romans Road.* Go through the plan of salvation called the Romans Road with your group. Have them mark their Bibles so that each passage has the next reference written by it. In this way they can walk someone easily through the plan of salvation. Mark Romans 3:10; 3:23; 6:23; 10:9, 10, 13.

Picking a Flick

BIG IDEA The movies we choose to watch not only reflect our values, but also influence them.

BIBLE INPUT Psalm 101

BRING: Bibles
Pencils
Paper
Popped popcorn (lots of it)

1 Stage a Popcorn Contest

Organize everyone into pairs, and give each pair a small amount of popcorn. Each pair can choose who is the thrower and who is the receiver. Direct receivers to stand at least six inches away from the throwers. The thrower should toss a piece of popcorn in the open mouth of the receiver (no hands allowed for the receiver). The team with the least popcorn on the floor at the end is the winner.

Another great way to play is to blindfold the throwers and let the receivers sound a consistent beep (or say anything they want) so that the thrower can take aim. As before, the least popcorn on the floor at the end makes a winning pair.

2 Eat and Talk

Divide into informal discussion groups and provide plenty of fresh popcorn for munchies. Guide the discussion with the following:

- **One of my favorite movies is. . . .**
- **The reason I like that movie is. . . .**
- **My favorite part of that movie is. . . .**
- **Why do you go to movies or rent them,? What does that kind of entertainment do for us?**
- **Do the movies we love affect the way we think? Give some examples.**
- **How do movies affect us emotionally?**
- **Describe the process you go through in a video store choosing movies.**
- **Do you have different standards for movies you see at the theater and videos that you rent? Describe the standards and any reasons behind them.**

3 Find Scriptural Guidelines

In order to do inductive Bible study in small groups, divide up and have each group write each verse from Psalm 101 on a separate sheet of paper (so you end up with a copy of the psalm for each group). Have the writers write large enough so that each verse fills the page. Line up the pages (tape them, if you have tape available) so that you have a large copy of the psalm. Then have each group use its copy to complete the following steps. (If you have colorful markers, use them.)

- Circle the word "eyes" everywhere it occurs.
- Underline each phrase starting with "I will . . ." including what the psalmist is saying he will do.
- Draw a lightning bolt (light enough so you can still read it) through the things or people that the psalmist wants to destroy or stay away from.

• Draw a smile by the things or people the psalmist wants to be like, or be close to.

Discuss how this psalm applies to the movies you watch. Use questions such as:

• **Why do you think David, the psalmist, wanted to stay away from evil so much?**

• **What kind of traits does this reveal about David?**

• **What movies would we consider contraband if our standards of who and what we are around were as high as David's?**

• **Does that mean we shouldn't watch anything that shows someone doing something wrong?** Guide the discussion toward the point that there is a difference between a movie showing human behavior and a movie glorifying evil.

• **Let's say you took David to the movies Friday night. Name some movies he'd probably get up and walk out of. Why?**

• **Name some movies David would probably sit through with you.**

• **Do you think David would want buttered popcorn or plain?** Loosen up. See what they say.

• **What keeps us from being as picky as David was about who and what he exposed himself to?**

Create a Movie Checklist

With the full group, create and write down a movie checklist. Below are some suggestions.

• **Does justice prevail?**
• **Does the movie leave me feeling hopeless?**
• **Does it cause me to take evil lightly?**
• **Do I observe a lot of behavior I'm trying to avoid?**
• **Do I find myself pulling for the bad guy?**
• **Am I tempted to do things I shouldn't?**
• **Are authority figures consistently represented as stupid?**

Movie Rating

To wrap up this session, have each kid rate one movie or video he or she watched this past week. Use the checklist you created in Step 4 or another rating system your kids come up with. For example, create a rating system along the lines of the one the movie industry uses: JP for Justice Prevails, WOB for Watch Out for Behavior, or TF for Temptation Factor.

Optional Extras

1. *Film Clips.* Have kids bring videotapes already cued to one of their favorite parts of a movie. Have each person give an introduction leading up to this point in the movie and telling why this part is his or her favorite.

2. *Moviemaking.* Borrow some videocameras and make some short clips representing scenes the kids think they should watch. Afterwards, talk about the differences between these scenes and scenes they think they shouldn't watch.

3. *Silent Movies.* Turn out the lights. Swing the beam of a flashlight quickly across one spot on the wall. Have volunteers go up and impersonate Charlie Chaplin or some such silent movie actor.

4. *Another Popcorn Game.* If you have time, play this game in Step 1. With tape mark a large square on the floor and divide that square into four quadrants. Divide the group into four teams and assign each team a quadrant. Place an equal amount of popcorn in the center of each quadrant. The object for each team is to keep their quadrant free of popcorn by blowing together and creating wind to clear the popcorn. No hands inside the square.

Making Political Choices

BIG IDEA

Each of us must decide which issues are important to us and support the people who best represent our views. Even those who aren't old enough to vote can benefit from being informed about candidates and the issues.

BIBLE INPUT

Romans 13:1-6
Micah 6:8

BRING:

Bibles
Pencils
Paper
Current newspapers,
  news magazines,
  political literature

1 *Pick an Animal*

We're going to talk about politics, which means we have to talk about politicians. If you had to pick an animal to represent the reputation of politicians in our country, what would you choose?

Together, come up with a definition of a politician. Discuss the different negative stereotypes people have about politicians. This session deals primarily with the two political parties in the United States. Feel free to adapt the steps to reflect your political system if you live outside the U.S.

• **Why do you think Republicans are represented by an elephant and Democrats by a donkey?** Your kids may come up with some creative answers. For the record, Andrew Jackson first used the donkey as a political symbol after his opponents called him a "jackass" in the 1828 campaign. In the 1880s, political cartoonist Thomas Nast drew a cartoon with a donkey representing the Democrats and the symbol caught on. The Republicans' story of the elephant isn't as funny. In 1874, the same Thomas Nast drew a political cartoon and used an elephant to represent the Republicans. That's it.

2 *Why? Because . . .*

Give each group member a piece of paper. Have kids tear the paper in half. On one half they should write a question beginning with "Why." (For example: Why did the chicken cross the road?) On the other half they should write the answer, beginning with "Because." (Because it wanted to prove to the raccoon that it could be done.)

Collect the papers, keeping all the why's together and all the because's together. Make sure both piles of paper are scrambled well.

Distribute the questions and answers so that each person has one of both, but not the ones that were written together. Then have each kid read the statements as if they went together.

After you laugh for a while, debrief with the following kinds of questions:

• **What was so funny about these statements as we read them?**

• **What is not funny about not getting straight answers to questions?**

• **What is dangerous about politicians not giving straight answers?**

• **Suppose you could ask the president one question. What would you ask him?** Let kids speculate for a couple of minutes. Encourage kids to think about some of the issues they feel are important.

Most people say they vote for the issues, not the person, but people often are loyal to one party because of that party's traditional views on certain issues.

3 Party Lines

As a group, make a list of some of the typical views of the two parties. For example, some people might associate Republicans with big business, the wealthy, and a strong military. Democrats might be associated with the disadvantaged, federal programs for the poor, and less military spending. Some may say that Republicans are generally more conservative and Democrats are liberal. Try to move beyond the labels to the types of issues each party supports.

Next, ask kids to decide which political party these Bible characters would belong to (if kids need some help with the characters, have volunteers look up the Scripture passages): The Rich Young Ruler —Matthew 19:16-23; Joseph—Genesis 41:41-49; Amos—Amos 5:11, 12; Zacchaeus—Luke 19:1-10, before and after.

It's fine if kids disagree as long as they give reasons for their answers.

• **What about Jesus? What party do you think He would have belonged to?** This could generate an interesting discussion. Jesus probably would have placed character issues and principles over particular political parties.

Actually, a politician's character and stand on the issues should be more important than his or her party affiliation.

4 God and Politics

In groups of twos and threes, have kids read Romans 13:1-6 and answer these two questions. Call the group back together to exchange ideas.

• **Suppose you decide to go into politics. How would this passage influence you?** (For starters, you wouldn't misuse your power since your right to rule has been established by God. You'd have to have a sense of right and wrong in order to judge other people's actions.)

• **As a citizen of this country, what are your political responsibilities?** (Verse 5 sums it up: ". . . submit to the authorities, not only because of possible punishment but also because of conscience.")

Let's add the word "Christian" in that last question. Do Christians have different political responsibilities? Point out that the difference is in how we view the issues. This doesn't mean there's always a Christian way to vote, but there is a biblical way of evaluating the issues, especially moral issues.

In fact, Micah 6:8 has three good guidelines. Read the verse aloud, pointing out the three guidelines: to act justly, to love mercy, and to walk humbly with God.

As you make up your mind about the issues, support the person who will work for justice, who will be compassionate, and who isn't power crazy. After all, no politician or government is beyond God's ultimate control.

5 *Election Day*

Schedule this session at a time when an election is coming up, or just took place. Vote for the same candidates as you hold this mock election.

Ask: **If the election were held today, who would you vote for?**

Hand out the same political literature, newspapers, and magazine articles (if any) about the candidates who are running for office, ask kids to weigh the pros and cons of each candidate, based on Micah 6:8 and Romans 13:1-6. Encourage kids to do a little campaigning if they'd like.

When kids have pretty much made up their minds, call for the vote. Have kids write down their vote. Tally the votes and declare the winner.

Afterward, take an exit poll and ask kids why they voted the way they did.

Optional Extras

1. *Elephants and Donkeys.* Invite several Republicans and several Democrats in for a panel discussion. Have kids ask them questions about why they support the party they do. Try to articulate some of the key differences between the two parties. Encourage kids to think for themselves and make their own decisions—especially when they are old enough to vote.

2. *Campaign Trail.* Divide your group into two political parties. Instruct them to come up with a name and a platform that consists of three goals for the youth group and how they would accomplish those goals. Each party should choose a candidate for youth group leader. Set up campaign speeches for the two candidates, stressing that they must influence as many people as possible on both sides to vote for them. After the candidates have made their speeches, you might want to have a vote for the candidate who was most convincing.